Word of

CW00386294

Word of Mouth

Using the remembered Bible
for building community

Janet Lees

WILD GOOSE PUBLICATIONS
THE IONA COMMUNITY

Copyright © Janet Lees

First published 2007 by
Wild Goose Publications,
4th Floor, Savoy House, 140 Sauchiehall St, Glasgow G2 3DH, UK.
Wild Goose Publications is the publishing division of the Iona Community.
Scottish Charity No. SCO03794. Limited Company Reg. No. SCO96243.
www.ionabooks.com

ISBN 978-1-905010-33-2

The publishers gratefully acknowledge the support of the Drummond Trust,
3 Pitt Terrace, Stirling FK8 2EY in producing this book.

Cover design © Wild Goose Publications

Janet Lees has asserted her right under the Copyright, Designs and Patents Act,
1988 to be identified as the author of this work.

All rights reserved. No part of this publication may be reproduced in any form
or by any means including photocopying or any information storage or retrieval
system, without written permission from the publisher.

A catalogue record for this book is available from the British Library.

Overseas distribution:
Australia: Willow Connection Pty Ltd, Unit 4A, 3-9 Kenneth Road, Manly
Vale, NSW 2093
New Zealand: Pleroma, Higginson Street, Otane 4170, Central Hawkes Bay
Canada: Novalis/Bayard Publishing & Distribution, 10 Lower Spadina Ave.,
Suite 400, Toronto, Ontario M5V 2Z2

Printed by Bell & Bain, Thornliebank, Glasgow

Contents

Acknowledgements

This book really happened. It contains real things from and for real life. These things came from the real lives of real people in real places. In the main that place was Sheffield, South Yorkshire, UK, and particularly Shiregreen and St James United Reformed Churches there. My thanks to all those who shared in the stuff that has become words, and more, here. Whilst most of these resources are new, a few have appeared elsewhere, although there may be subtle word differences between versions, if only because 'life's like that'.

This book is dedicated with thanks to Bob and Hannah for being my daily companions.

Preface

This book is about a story. Although the story is an old one, it is about how it was made real in the lives of people alive today. That was a shared experience and, in telling about it here, I am not claiming it as mine. Rather I am telling it from my point of view. Others might recount it differently: stories are like that.

For the five years or so described here I was exploring what it meant to be involved in the mission of some small churches in the city of Sheffield. The story is not just about churches and the people of all ages in them but they are part of the tale. It is about the communities with which those churches engage in ministry and mission. It was a hard journey and, like any other, required resources in order to keep going. This book describes some of the biblical resources, home-grown in this particular place, that sustained us.

The book begins with the essentially wacky idea that we might use a version of the Bible that is not written down. This idea has its origins in a work on biblical interpretation with people who have communication difficulties, of which there are plenty both in the church and in society. The method relies on collaborative work within the group to build up shared remembered versions of biblical texts. The narrative of the life of Jesus and the responses of his followers and friends is the core story of this remembered gospel.

A closer look at the life of Jesus and the fullness of his humanity reveals that here is one who spent his whole life with marginalised people, or 'on the edge'. His story comes alive as the group remembers it together. The ordinary life stories of the members of the group gradually come out of silence as participants begin to recognise the connections between the remembered gospel and their own lives. So telling the story and interpreting the story become inextricably linked.

This book is in three parts. Each part has an exploration of the gospel in a remembered form and life on the margins as joint interests. It begins with a description of how to use a remembered oral version of the Bible with groups of different sorts. It includes a series of remembered Bible studies and some reflections and activities based around working with remembered Bibles.

Part two is about some particular bits of the Bible: the edges. By this I mean genres and characters that occur in the Bible but which are not usually the main focus of attention. Considering the Bible from the edges is a way of using it with people who live on the edges of our society. Using parables is an example of this strategy. This form of story found in the gospels is explored and retold here: 'played with' for greater fun, accessibility and relevance. It is followed by some stories of people from the edges of the Bible: those less well known or even unnamed.

Part three uses the language, the images and the ideas that we have gathered from our remembered gospels and makes them into words for worship: prayers, hymns and meditations. There are three main themes in these worship resources. The first is concerned with the God we meet every day: 'Mondays God'. We meet God at the garage, on the way to school, at the bus stop, in the post office queue. This God is not different from the God we meet on Sundays. Telling the story of the everyday God is a prayerful activity, hence the second theme: 'Show me the life'. This is the Jesus Christ of the streets. He is the One who is intimately involved with our lives. And, thirdly, Jesus calls us to follow and so the final theme is 'Travelling on': the adventure continues.

Although this book could not have been written without the company of other people, I accept responsibility for the way I have reflected and interpreted that journey here. I am grateful to those who agreed that I could include their versions of stories we had remembered together. I hope that those who have shared the journey will recognise the common ground we have covered. Their company has been inspirational as 'from the old we travel to the new'.[1]

Janet Lees
November 1st, All Saints, 2005
Sheffield, South Yorkshire, and Hadfield, Derbyshire.

---

[1] Words from a hymn by Sydney Carter (1912–2004).

Part one

Bible studies without Bibles

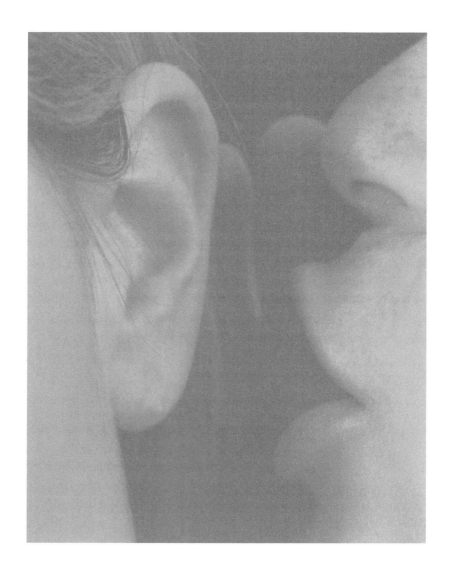

Chapter one

Bible studies without Bibles

It is quite nonsensical, unrealistic, impractical and brainless – in other words wacky – to suggest we can do Bible studies without Bibles. Well, without written Bibles anyway. To make links between lived experience and the Bible in order to develop a more chaotic spirituality that is like the real world, we shall use not a written Bible but a remembered one. When Lorraine says:

> *If I was going to preach a sermon it would be about 'the Good Samaritan' or what's that other one [pause], yeah, the one about 'whoever has not sinned should cast the first stone'; that one* [1]

she is using a remembered Bible, not a written one. Between August 1998 and January 2004 we used remembered versions of the Bible together in some small churches in north-east Sheffield. The methods we have developed to do this and some of the consequences of such wacky ways will be described and discussed in these first two chapters. To begin, a group of people from those churches introduce themselves and the context:

> *We are a group of small churches in the north of Sheffield at the heart of deprivation, poverty and unemployment, with a wide diversity of races and cultures in our area. Struggle is what we are used to as churches and communities.* [2]

Using remembered versions of the Bible here has developed into a pedagogy: a way of teaching and learning (see more about this on pages 48–50). It is a particular kind of teaching and learning: one in which both teachers and students take an equal responsibility, one in which the central task is to empower the powerless to emerge from the passivity and dependency that currently seems characteristic of life in many UK churches. A critical pedagogy

- is created in collaboration with others;
- aims to liberate, make whole, challenge and change the oppressive status quo;
- is carried out on the edge, in the borderlands, at the frontier.

Clearly there are some advantages and disadvantages in using remembered versions of Bible stories in worship, study groups and community work. Amongst the obvious advantages are that most people join in. But there is more to it than that. Evaluating the process of using remembered versions of the Bible with some users revealed the following points: [3]

1. We can think of stories we like. This advantage was first suggested by some young people aged 8-11 years and suggests that they had found it a good way to get into the Bible. When exploring what is in your remembered Bible, begin with the stories you like. See what you remember of those and ask yourselves why. A favourite story of the group was 'The Good Samaritan', because 'we can relate to it. It helps us understand how to make a better world'. So a strategy suggested by children developed into one embraced by adults and that brings us neatly to the next point.

2. It is a good technique to use with all ages, because all can contribute to it equally.

3. However, to begin with it can seem intimidating. Various people admitted to initial feelings of panic, although most also agreed that their fears were not eventually borne out, or gave way to other more positive feelings as we went along. There was agreement that the process helped the group to realise how much there is in the Bible and that was considered comforting. It was also said that there were 'stories inside you influencing your life'. So you might start off with panic but you soon 'realise you do know it'.

4. Using this method the Bible becomes an everyday book. The more informal language of storytelling that is involved means that people can easily tell the stories again in other situations. It helps to make connections between the Bible stories and daily life and demonstrates that there are issues of daily life in each Bible story.

5. Compared with a passive listening approach in worship, this method stopped people switching off. Moreover, it was a sign that we are here to learn and was a way of moving the church on in learning. It indicated a belief that learning was for everyone, not just children. However, it is important to note that even in a group that has used this approach for some time, not everyone – for whatever reasons – seems comfortable with this, affirms this view or joins in.

6. It exposes you to other people's opinions about the Bible. Discussing the remembered versions with other people is a way of sharing knowledge and understanding. This helped people who started out hesitantly to gain more confidence.

7. Remembering the Bible is an example of learning by doing. It is generally agreed that we learn more easily by doing rather than just listening. Repetition has a part in this process. As we get more familiar with stories, we become more confident in telling and interpreting them. Although at first it might seem that repetition can lead to increased boredom as in 'I've heard that before', participants actually found that each repetition was different, coloured by various people's interpretations. Being exposed to the varied views of different people was a good thing that made the group think more about familiar pieces.

8. It fires the imagination. There are many other creative activities that can develop from remembering the Bible together (see pages 23 & 24), using a range of media like art, sewing, and drama.

9. It is fun and interactive. This may be unusual in some churches, or may be confined to certain times and places rather than breaking out unpredictably any time. The group might find it needs to give itself permission to enjoy the process. What we are used to may influence how we behave or respond in church.

10. It is like being back at school. A small number of adults have been known to respond with this kind of comment, even if not when with the whole group. However, it has been said often enough to confirm that it is sometimes an issue and something the facilitator needs to bear in mind. The proportion of people with this view in the congregation may heavily influence the success of the process. Clearly it is difficult to remember what you have not heard, although frequent repetition can help to overcome some of this. The facilitator needs to be careful not to 'put people on the spot' or seem threatening or patronising in other ways. The educational experiences of individuals in the group may influence whether or not they come to activities like this in a positive or negative frame of mind.

Therefore there are strategies that have been found to help people to join in the remembering process. These include:

- begin by sharing what people remember informally in a small group;
- choose a story which has repetitive bits so that people can join in

> gradually;

- ask a small group to prepare the remembering in advance;
- use an informal setting rather than a formal one;
- suggest clues from picture Bibles, films, musicals, plays, a cartoon, a painting;
- provide an outline of the story to fill in the details;
- try it more than once, even if it does not seem easy the first time.

If you use these methods, try not to worry that people will remember the wrong thing, or get it wrong in some other way. It is true that sometimes details get mixed up or missed out in the remembering. Everyone remembers things differently and the way memories are stored in our brains will differ. One person's version of a remembered text is likely to be different from another's, but that does not make it wrong. Where people draw in parts of other episodes, it can be helpful to explore together why they remember these things. The process is trying to give people confidence to use the Bible as they have remembered it. Therefore the facilitator and the group members should try to encourage rather than discourage participants.

It is possible that on occasions an important bit gets forgotten. Of course, that begs the question of how an important bit is defined. But if something does seem to have been left out there are several approaches the facilitator might take:

- wait for a while, as silence is not a waste of time;
- prompt the group gently, as in a big group there is often somebody who remembers, even if only sketchily;
- leave it out this time, as it may get remembered another day;

If all this sounds a bit risky, then that is the essence of using the 'remembering the Bible' process. Hopefully you will find that some interesting discussions take place at the edges of memory. Not having everything scripted in advance allows more opportunity for new or unexpected things to appear. Using remembered versions has given me a different view of the written versions. There must have been many versions of gospel stories doing the rounds at the time. Some got written down; the rest were forgotten but they were not worthless.

Some groups will hate using remembered texts. In our largely literate society the printed Bible has become indispensable for some groups, and they will find it very difficult or impossible to put it away. Do not assume that your group will be like this, but you may need to be ready to make allowances; some people like the back-up of the written text somewhere (you can always read a written version aloud after the shared remembering if you prefer). If you want to use these methods, then the leadership team needs to:

- agree in advance who might be good at starting the group off on remembering these episodes from Jesus's life story;
- prepare material that will give people clues about the stories to be remembered;
- be gentle and take sufficient time for the task (both preparation and during worship).

It can take some time to reconstruct a remembered text with a group and may include lots of silences. Try not to rush them: once again silence is not a waste of time. It is a huge generalisation to say that 'there is a Bible in everyone', and even seems to go against the popular view of contemporary British culture, but this method has been tried and tested in many different groups.

Methods of making a remembered text

There are many ways of making a remembered version with a group. Some are outlined here and others are used in the series of remembered Bible studies on page 33. You will probably think of others as you develop the technique in your own context. The ones here have been used with groups of different sizes, from two to two hundred people, although if the group is very large then some initial small group work is probably helpful. Small group work does not need to be formal but may just mean talking to the few people sitting next to you. However, it can also mean moving the furniture, which can readily turn into a sort of chaos, depending on the space, the people and the furniture.

Each method will be illustrated here with an example. If trying this yourself, it is probably best to begin with one of the more memorable episodes from the gospels – for example the feeding of the five thousand, the parable of the Good Samaritan, the story of Zaccheus – so the group can see that they can do it.

Flip chart outline method. On a flip chart list the main episodes of the story in the form of up to about half a dozen headings that represent the beginning, middle and end of the story. Then invite the group to fill in each section.

For example, for the story of Jesus being baptised, three headings might be:

- John the Baptist is at work: where? doing what?
- Jesus arrives: what happens?
- Afterwards: how does it end?

This has proved to be a very rich story, as Jennifer's version demonstrates:

When Jesus was baptised it was a sunny day. There were a lot of people and his mum and dad came late. Jesus was already there because he had camped there. The man that baptised him was John. I bet it was exciting and Jesus probably told one of his stories. [4]

One of the most important initial aims of the process is demonstrated here: getting started. Here the beginning, middle and end of the story are rather different from the versions in the written gospels but there are links to the gospel story and to Jennifer's own experience. The story of Jesus's baptism is often repeated and provides a good starting point for remembering his ministry in many creative ways (see pages 60–61).

Finish-off-the-sentence method. Have a version of the story written out on cards in single sentences that are left unfinished. Present the sentences in order and invite the group to finish off each sentence as they think appropriate. This method is helpful if you fear no one will remember anything.

For example, some sentences about the story of the Wedding at Cana might be:

- Jesus went to a/the wedding and …
- His mother said to him …
- He replied to her …
- Then he …
- Afterwards, the head of the household said …

Animated method. Have some toys, cut-outs or puppets to represent the characters of the story and invite some members of the group to move these around as directed by other members of the group. In small groups you might want to suggest that one group thinks about the activities of one character whilst another group does another character, etc.

Rehearsed method. Ask people to look at the story in advance of the occasion when you want to use it and come ready to retell it to each other. This is another good method for the group that thinks it cannot do this, or will not like doing it, but are willing to do some homework.

Picture method. Use a picture Bible, some cartoons illustrating the main events of the story, or even a reproduction of a well-known painting representing the events, as a trigger to help people remember. You might want to draw a large cartoon on the wall or do a mural, which is after all a centuries-old way of representing the Bible.

Storyteller method. This is for the group who remember nothing and who hate joining in. Find one or two people from the group who are willing to tell the story in their own words, either to small groups or the whole group. This can be followed by a time when the group(s) retell what they have heard to each other.

Charades method. The group animator provides a charade of the story to be remembered and people shout out responses as this progresses. This needs to begin in time-honoured charade fashion with a clue to what sort of episode it is. For a parable, cup your hands to your ears; for a miracle, sound a dramatic action 'da-da'; for a sad story, look sad, and happy for a happy one, etc.

Begin each 'episode' or 'bit' of the story separately and allow people opportunity to shout out what they think you are doing. You will need to over-act. This method is usually very chaotic.

For example, the parable of the sower needs to begin with a reminder that this is a parable and the title has two words: 'the' and 'sower' should then be acted out in turn ('the' is traditionally done by making the shape of a capital T with the hands). Once the group has got this, go on to act out the first line 'There was a sower sowing seeds'. After something like the expected response has been offered, go on to the second line – 'some seed fell on the footpath' – and continue all the way through. Make sure the 'birds of the air' are particularly dramatic, gruesome or comic, like the vultures in *Bedknobs and Broomsticks*. Dainty birds do not really have a place in this sort of drama. This has led to the story being renamed the 'Parable of the Squawking Birds'. [5] Similarly, the bit where the seeds get choked to death by the sun and keel over needs to be overplayed for full effect.

This has become something of a favourite at Shiregreen United Reformed Church, where members of the group now say, 'I remember this one,' and even discuss it with people they have only just met as an example of 'how to do remembered texts'.

Another way of doing this, perhaps the second or third time round (lectionaries are like this!), is to get the group to take the different parts in as impromptu a way as possible. One side can be the rocks where the seeds fall, the other side the brambles and thorns. Invite people to explore 'how to be a rock' or 'how to be a bramble'. This usually proves to be fairly chaotic. Others can be the birds, the seedlings, the sun, and so on.

Go for it method. Just go for it and see what happens. Invite people in small or large groups to discuss what they remember of the story. After they have done this, one person can collect up their responses episode by episode, checking with other groups/people to see what level of agreement is reached. The whole agreed version can be retold at the end. When bringing together the bits of the remembered text, try to be affirming, particularly of those who rarely offer a contribution or of anything different or unusual. This is the riskiest method and usually takes the longest.

Remember that the idea is to produce something you have remembered together – not a word for word version of any particular written translation but something that has come from the group's response to how the story is recalled by them all.

You may want to finish your remembered text with the response

> This is to us the Gospel of Christ.
> **Praise to Christ our Lord.**

or a song like 'Halle-halle-halle-lu-u-jah'. [6]

Remembering around a theme

One way of getting into remembering but not going straight for a specific text is to ask people to remember around a theme. For example, if the text to be remembered is the parable of the unforgiving servant, you might note in your preparation that it is prefaced by the question attributed to Peter about 'How often should I forgive?' This could be an opportunity to begin the remembering session with a short buzz on the question: How many examples of 'forgiving', both words and actions, can we remember from the gospels? The list generated might include: [7]

- Jesus on the cross;
- The story of Zaccheus;
- The story of the woman taken in adultery;
- The parable of the prodigal son;
- The Lord's Prayer.

It may also happen that during this introduction both the question and its answer – 'Not seven times but seventy times seven' – and the parable itself are mentioned. This gives the worship leader an opportunity to check in advance if this text is memorable or not, and therefore decide whether or not to proceed with a remembering of the specific text, or to continue by reading it aloud or retelling it instead. It also allows some preparation for the 'response' part of the worship, sometimes called a sermon in those groups that go in for lengthy monologues. If you are quick off the mark, note down some of the points made (or ask someone else to do this), and invite participants to discuss these further later on. This is one example of the way in which remembering a text quickly leads into interpreting a text.

Remembering exact words

The point of using remembered versions is not historical accuracy to one written translation or another, or even the original Greek. Some participants may remember like this and their contribution is to be welcomed. The extent to which this style of remembering is common across the whole group will depend on context. However, the remembering process is not for show-offs or anyone who wants to dominate the group. From time to time there will be a participant or two who is picky with someone else's version. It is important to encourage people to own their versions. Phrases like 'In my remembered version there's …' are to be commended. When someone says 'I've had it explained to me as …' ask if they agree or disagree with that explanation. It can often be helpful to point out differences in the written versions where these exist as a way of validating the differences in the remembered versions across a whole group. Occasionally exact words from a particular translation or written version will be remembered. This can be acknowledged and included in the whole process.

Advanced remembering

If you do this a lot, you may find it becomes quite fun and even enjoy-able. Then you are ready for advanced remembering. Sometimes there's more than one passage of scripture appointed by the lectionary that seems memorable. When this happens it seems a shame not to have a go at remembering both passages. Take, for example, the week at St James when we remembered two different things. From the Old Testa-ment we had Elijah running away to a cave. From the gospels we had Jesus healing a man, featuring some evil spirits and a herd of pigs. The whole group was not more than 16 people (aged 7–94) so the easiest thing to do was to suggest two groups: one to work on remembering the Elijah passage and the other the healing of the man, and the herd of pigs. Then each group took it in turns to tell the other group what they had remembered. In a bigger group there could be more than one smaller group working on each passage, and then for the retelling they could team up with a group who had worked on the opposite passage. After which it would be a good idea to leave a bit of space for anything interesting that came out of the remembering process to be shared in the whole group. The remembering process readily moves into an interpreting process. This is an important feature of using remembered methods and there is no need to stifle this. Encourage participants to make links between what they have remembered and real life situa-tions. Make the time as flexible as possible and be ready to see what participants contribute.

After using these remembered methods consistently for over five years (and that may seem a long time) these congregations were able to do it readily. As time went on people became more confident and thereby contributed even more. Within any group there are those who almost always speak and those who almost never do. There are no prizes for being either but over time it has been interesting to see what has happened. Whilst people who always speak probably continue to do so, the contribution of those who are quieter is now more apparent. It can be difficult to get loud people to listen to quiet ones. It can also be diffi-cult to encourage quiet ones to risk speaking out to loud ones. The group facilitators need to keep alert to the undercurrents in the group. Whilst small group work might usually be informal, sometimes it can help to arrange groups so that all the loud people are in one, and can thus shout at each other to their hearts' content, while all the quiet people are in others, giving them more space and time to express themselves in their preferred ways.

The family from Bethany [8]

One of the remembered texts I have often invited people to use is about the family at Bethany: Martha, Mary and Lazarus. Responses from several workshops and worship sessions remembering this family are included here as a way of introducing issues that come up when remembered texts are used, and how they might be handled. These comments come from work with groups from various places (Sheffield, Glasgow, East Midlands), of various sizes (from less than ten to over seventy people), of various ages (from toddlers to nonagenarians) and all abilities (including people described as having learning and communication difficulties).

Remembering who?

'A noisy one and a quiet one.'
The first memory people usually have about this family are the two sisters: one was noisy and one was quiet. It is this stereotype which has been at the heart of most interpretations and which needs liberating.

'I can't remember who went to prepare the dinner.'
Not everyone remembers names. When people work in groups, the aim is to get them to co-operate in order to share what they remember, rather than one or two thinking they know it all and dominating the discussion. What we do not remember is as important as what we do.

'One of them poured oil over his feet. Martha or Mary? We'll go for Mary.'
'I'm not sure which one came to the graveside. Does it matter?'
Not remembering names can lead on to not remembering who did what. Again let the group share knowledge rather than have individuals rise to the urge to tell everyone what they know. However, this kind of confusion can also provide an opportunity to discuss the reliability of the written text, where it came from and the role of remembering in its original formation.

'There was another mention of Lazarus and a rich man.'
There are often people with similar names in other parts of the Bible. Again, see this as an opportunity to discover what else people remember and why, rather than saying, 'We're not doing that one today.'

Remembering where?

'I think the Luke 10 one is probably the one she means.'
First there is the location in the written biblical text. Some people may know this, others will not. It is not necessarily important to know it. One person did tell me that 'you saying it was in Matthew or John didn't help me', so I rarely give the location of the written version unless asked or unless I am trying to point out differences between different people's versions. If the group are having difficulty coming to an agreed version, it can help to know that those to whom the written gospels are attributed rarely agreed on everything.

'A mile and a half down the road from the Mount of Olives.'
Then there is the geographical location. This may help some people. Equally there may be some who have visited the places and will have a reflection they can add.

'It's funny there is no mention of them [the family] at the crucifixion.'
In a remembered version there are no clear boundaries for where the story begins and ends like there are in the written text with its chapters and verses. Invite participants to decide for themselves and see what happens. This can be used to begin a discussion of the structure of the written version if that is relevant.

Remembering what?

'Mary said: My house is different. My brother is different. He lets me be different. He lets me learn and listen.'
Not being tied to a written version allows participants to retell the story in more liberating ways. Allow time for these imagined versions to be heard.

'He was useless and he went and died.'
For some participants it is enough to state baldly what silences there are in the story.

'I was not a well man. My name was never mentioned because I was never there.'

'Lazarus said: I've not said a lot. My sisters keep the family on an even keel. I went and died. I'm a bloke with not many choices in life.'

For others, those silences soon become something that can be opened up and examined, depending on their lived experiences. This can be a tender, poignant, painful and emotional process, so there needs to be time and space for affirmative listening when this is happening.

Remembering why?

'I don't think much was said about the brother.'

'Angry, angry! I think Jesus was angry in the story.'

'And Jesus said a short prayer and Lazarus came to life again and everyone was gobsmacked.'

These comments emerged from a workshop with people with learning and communication difficulties. The remembered text method is not just about reconstructing a text, although it begins there. In most groups it quickly develops into interpretation as participants consider what happened in the light of their own experiences. These participants revealed an important insight into the structure of the story:

Beginning	Middle	End
silence about Lazarus	Lazarus dies	silence about Lazarus

People who were often assumed to be silent could identify with the huge silences in this story about the presence and role of a key character: the silent Lazarus.

Not remembering

'I've never heard of them.'

'We don't remember anything about that.'

This can be true and, if so, it's important to handle the situation so that people do not feel they have been set up to fail. If it looks as if there may be bigger gaps in the collective memory than you hoped, then check this out by asking the whole group 'Who remembers this?' If there are those who do remember and those who do not, invite the groups to mix up a bit: move around so that each group contains some people who do remember and some who do not. Try not to make too many assumptions about who this will be. A seven-year-old may be as likely as a seventy-year-old. Using remembered versions in all-age sessions may look risky but the ensuing chaos can be creative. Even if we remember nothing from the Bible, we may have learnt that we did not need to stay in the same seats all the way through the session after all.

Here is a remembered version of the story of the family from Bethany:

> *In Bethany, Jesus turns up at tea-time. Martha panics. There is no food and she wants to do her best. Martha wants to do what is right and Mary winds her up. Mary gets distracted and Martha gets distracted. Martha loses her temper and there's the usual sibling rivalry stuff. Martha says to Jesus: 'Don't you care?' Jesus says to Martha: 'Martha, Martha, you are worried about many things.' Martha says to Jesus: 'I knew you'd take her side.'*

Observe what the remembered version puts in and leaves out. Interpretation has immediately become part of the remembering as this group picks up the idea that family relationships and sibling rivalry are at the heart of what was going on here. This is a refreshing idea, because it gets us away from the old stereotypes mentioned earlier about 'the noisy one and the quiet one'. After all, neither of the sisters, in the traditional interpretation, presents a very liberating role model. Whilst the line 'Martha, Martha, you are worried …' is lifted more or less from the written text (and this does happen from time to time), the final line – 'Mary has chosen the better part' – is omitted here.

> *Busy Creator, Silent Son,*
> *Dancing Spirit, three in one:*
> *from silent tombs you call us out,*
> *give us life and join our shout.*
> *Alleluia!*

Remember that? a series of remembered Bible studies

If you want to try this method, but think that maybe it would be best to do it with a small group first, rather than with the whole worshipping congregation, or you just want to see some of the different ways of doing it set out like a recipe, here is a short series of remembered Bible studies which can be used for the former purpose but also acts as the latter. The main aim of this series is to show that you can still use the Bible as a springboard for mission even if you have a communication difficulty (and remember, we all have those now and again). The series is in four parts, each one involving a different way of working with remembered texts. The particular texts have been chosen both for being in some way memorable and to illustrate some particular point in respect of contemporary mission on the edge of the church.[9] The leadership team preparing the series may want to consult some written versions, some commentaries, documentaries, etc, as background information.[10] Each Bible study is intended to fit into an hour to an hour and a half time slot, so the group has plenty of time.

Beginning to remember

You may want to do a short introductory exercise to convince people they can use remembered versions of the Bible. This may include outlining some of the principles of working with remembered versions which were mentioned at the beginning of this section, like being collaborative rather than competitive. I sometimes begin by inviting responses to 'all the women mentioned in the gospels' or 'all the silent people', or any other particularly relevant theme for the group you are working with. Or you could use the Jesus life-line activity on page 60. Remember to remove any printed versions of the Bible from the group's possession before starting these studies, so no one feels tempted to 'just look it up'. In the four Bible studies presented here the 'just go for it method' is the method of choice when constructing the remembered text. This can be substituted by any of the other methods that the group might cope with better. However, just going for it has the advantage of being very real and usually quite chaotic.

1. The nine unhealed lepers

In the first session it is important to be able to demonstrate to people that they can in fact remember the Bible. The story of ten people who had leprosy and were healed by Jesus appears well known enough as a starting point. But other well-known incidents could be substituted: the paralysed person who goes through the roof would also be a good story to begin with. The two things to try to achieve in this session are:

- to produce a remembered version of the incident;
- to consider some of the silences at the edges of the story.

The titles of these studies have been chosen to provoke people to explore beyond the usual familiar interpretations. Although, in worship, it is not usually necessary or appropriate to write down every remembered version, it can be an important way of showing participants that they can remember the Bible. Provide small groups of 3-5 people with a large sheet of paper and a thick marker pen. Then give them time to discuss between themselves what they remember of the story, and write it down on the sheet provided. This might take up to 20 minutes or so, depending on how big the groups are, how much they stay on task and so on. Don't worry during this time. Wander around listening to what is coming up in the groups – and something will be. Make a note of anything that you can use to illustrate points in the remembering process later on, like those given earlier on pages 19-20.

When the remembered versions have been written down put them up around the walls of the room and invite everyone to look at them. Encourage the group to help each other where this poses a difficulty for any participants. Here is a selection of versions produced by groups that illustrates something of what can come up during this process.

Version one
Once upon a time ...
There were ten lepers who asked Jesus to heal them.
One of them was a Samaritan?
Jesus healed them all – and told them to go to the priest to confirm their cure. Off they went.
After the healing was confirmed, one of them only returned to

thank Jesus (? the Samaritan).

Jesus asked: 'Where are the other nine?'

Version two

Jesus was walking past a place where ten lepers were living. Ten of them had heard about Jesus, and came to him to ask for healing. Jesus healed them and ordered them to show themselves to the priest, according to the Law of Moses. Only one returned to say thank you. Jesus asked: 'Where are the other nine?'

Version three

Jesus was going from Samaria to Galilee when ten lepers (ringing bells) ran towards him. They asked to be healed saying, ''Elp, verily we feel 'orrible.' Jesus said: 'Go and show yourselves to the priest

One day as Jesus was walking along the road with his disciples he was met by ten men (people) with a dreaded skin disease.

'Lord, make us clean' they said

'Go and show yourselves to the priest and make the sacrifice laid down by Moses' Jesus replied.

As they were going they realised with they were clean. One was so full of joy he ran back to Jesus to thank him.

Jesus said, 'Were there not ten cleansed where are the other nine?' Only one has come to give thanks and he is a Samaritan.

and make the offering laid down by the Law.' So off they went.

As they were going, one turned back and knelt before Jesus, giving thanks, and saying, 'Verily, I feel 'orrible no more.' Jesus said: 'Were not ten healed? Why was only one found to give thanks – and he a Samaritan?'

Version four

Each group has managed to produce a remembered version and they are all, including the picture version, remarkably similar in content. Point these things out to the group. Point out also any major differences; for example, some mention that one person was a Samaritan; others do not mention this. If they had thought about it but not included it, this may be one of the silences around this story.

The main silence in the story concerns what happened to the other nine, although there may be other silences mentioned by participants, like what happened as they went along the road, what later happened to the one who did come back, and so on. Encourage people to name some of the silences and if possible explore some with storytelling either in small groups or with 'something prepared earlier'. The story of the women with the yeast (page 104) originally featured at this point as a way of drawing this session to a close.

2. The insulted woman

Sometimes called 'the Syro-Phoenician woman' or 'the Canaanite woman', this anonymous female person is probably best known for her dogs. The suggestion that the reference to the dogs was an insult on Jesus's part does not go down well in all kinds of church. In the sort of churches where Jesus can only be your best mate if he is also so sugary sweet as to be completely unreal it can be hard for people to consider that Jesus could have insulted someone and then changed his mind about something. These are two of the possible silences to be explored in remembering this story.

Invite participants to remember the story in small groups of 3–5 members. Once again, go around listening in on groups as they do this, collecting up anything that might need referring to later. It is usually interesting with this story to find different interpretations of Jesus's response to the woman and vice versa. When each group has a version they are willing to own, then get the whole group back together again and ask one group to start the story off. Go around the groups collecting one episode at a time to build up the story. If differences emerge between groups, then try to hold these up for the whole group to examine and agree on a final version. When a version of the story has been agreed, then invite comments or discussion to identify any silences and any contemporary parallels that group members may have thought of. This might include:

- confronting a member of the health services about malpractice;
- seeing a head teacher about your child being excluded from school;
- dealing with a racial insult from a public service provider;
- struggling to establish your disabled child's right to inclusive education.

Invite people to re-form the small groups. Provide a large sheet of paper and some marker pens to each group and invite them to make a cartoon reflecting what for them is the 'punch-line' of the story in visual form. Encourage them to try to make the link between the story and the contemporary social world in their cartoons.

If cartoons are not so easy to use with your group, then try a song or a rap instead in the second part. Once again, try to encourage people to explore some of the silences in the story through this medium. Depending on which method you use, close the session with a gallery time when people look at the cartoons, or a talent show when the songs and raps are presented.

3. The family from Bethany

I have already illustrated some of the issues that arise from discovering the family from Bethany in remembered texts (see pages 29–32). There should, if possible, always be room in a Bible study series for this family. Begin by inviting people to get into threes. Then ask them to think about what they remember of Martha, Mary and Lazarus. This should be a fairly quick-fire three or four minutes rather than long and drawn out; 'just to start the ball rolling', as it were. It is possible that there will be one or more members of a group who have never heard of this trio. This can be dealt with in various ways:

- once ideas about who they were are shared by the whole group, this may provide enough to kick-start even the group with the least collective memory;
- participants may change to another group to spread the collective memory around a bit – there are no rules which say you have to stay in the same group all the way through.

Be creative and let the group find ways of overcoming what might seem like an obstacle.

In the second phase invite each trio to remember the story of Martha, Mary and Lazarus as they can. This can turn out to be a number of different things:

- a version of Jesus at the house in Bethany at which Martha does lunch and Mary listens – Lazarus is silent (though not necessarily absent);
- a version of Jesus returning to Bethany after the death of Lazarus, leading on to the raising of Lazarus;
- a combination of the two;
- something else!

For the third phase you may want to provide some thought-provoking input about silent women and men, particularly the role of people with disabilities in the society of first-century Palestine. You might want to contrast this with some information about the lives of people with disabilities and their families today. What I am leading up to here is the implication that some, or all, the members of this family were marginalised due to social attitudes to disability, and that people with disabilities are still marginalised in the church and more widely.

Two sisters live with an unmarried brother. It is an unusual family unit in a society in which almost all adult males would have married. Unmarried women would have found a home with married brothers but unmarried men were rare, unless they were marginalised for some other reason. Lazarus does not speak in the written gospel accounts of this family and he dies in unspoken circumstances. It could be hypothesised that he had an impairment or was disabled. A variety of common circumstances might include learning difficulties or epilepsy, both alluded to in other gospel accounts.

For the fourth phase, invite each trio to take the part of one of the siblings, Martha, Mary and Lazarus, so that each group has one of each family member. Participants are then asked to role-play what is going on in this family, paying particular attention to the silences. This can be done with a few props and even in the suggested style of a TV 'soap'.

4. The missiologically challenged followers

In this last of the four studies we will use a story that clearly has two parts. The two parts are usually used separately but here we will combine them in order to let each speak differently. Groups using these techniques often say, 'We couldn't do this; we've got pews in our church!' [11] Whilst it may be more challenging in some ways because the whole pew thing is usually a signal that a church prefers formality and is not into close contact, it can be done in such venues provided there is a will. One way is just to get the people to talk to each other where they are. Of course, this is tricky if no one is sitting within speaking distance of each other, but equally they could be asked to move. It may be necessary to provide an incentive for them to move out of their pews, in which case a packet of biscuits might help. If the space is divided into two halves by a centre aisle, then this two-part remembering task works well, with each half remembering a different bit.

So, split the group into two roughly even halves to begin. Invite people to talk with their nearest neighbours about their part of the story. The 'one story in two parts' is the episode on the mountain of the Transfiguration and the healing of the boy with epilepsy. [12] These two incidents are recorded one after the other in the written gospels. Have one half of the group concentrate on the first part: Jesus and the three disciples up on the mountain. If necessary provide some clues where you think they may help remembering. These could be written clues, or pictures, or just a few things said at the commencement of the process. The other half of the group needs to remember what happens at the bottom of the mountain, when Jesus meets a boy with epilepsy and his family. Again a few clues might be in order for this one.

When the two groups have established a version they are ready to own, then invite each half to tell their story to the other, starting with up the mountain and finishing with down the mountain. Once the story has been told, invite participants to explore some of the silences that they have encountered in their group work. If necessary feed in here some of the things you have overheard going on in the groups in the first part.

Give out some large sheets of paper and marker pens. Let the group decide how this will work rather than splitting into groups. If the seating is fixed, then they will probably use common sense, but some may surprise you and move around to join in, eat the biscuits or opt out! Draw the group's attention to the way in which newspaper headline writers condense a story to a few well-chosen words reflecting the particular social issues they think will interest their readership. Have a few examples ready if necessary. Each group can now put their version of this story into a headline according to a particular newspaper, magazine or interest group. Once again, remind the group to explore ways into the silences in this story. The boy does not speak – nor does his mother. How do participants explain that and what the story might have been like from their perspectives? The story on page 109, 'Downhill to Jerusalem', is told from the mother's point of view and could be used here. Conclude the session with a few well-read headlines that the groups have produced.

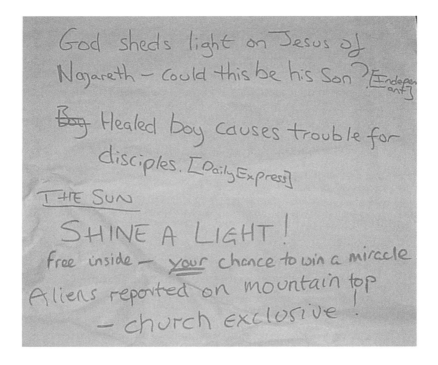

Pick and mix

The techniques used with these four Bible studies could be used with other texts or could be moved around within these four texts, depending on the particular group. The cartoon-drawing method works well with the family from Bethany. One group produced a cartoon of Martha greeting Jesus with the words 'You're late; your dinner's in the bin and Lazarus is dead!'

Equally the role-playing can be done with the Transfiguration and the family of the boy with epilepsy, again in two halves with one group sharing their findings with the other. Or you may use a different healing episode for the role-playing method: like the group who remembered Jairus's daughter as 'Natalie, the girl who didn't eat enough to keep a gnat alive' with a 'soap' episode about eating disorders. The main things to remember about the process are:

- expect it to be more chaotic than traditional Bible study (whatever that is), where the most chaotic bit is often finding the page number in the first place;
- expect the group to be able to do it, to remember the story and use it creatively together;
- listen hard as the session facilitator, feed in what you hear and leave time – and silence – for things to happen;
- leave plenty of spaces for participants to comment, think, reflect and share in their thoughts about the remembered texts and about the process itself;
- enjoy it.

Not just for children

It is not unusual for the unenlightened to suggest that this method is 'just for children'. Whilst children can and do take part in it, it is not reserved for them alone. I still get far too many invitations for my liking to churches where I am expected to do 'a children's talk'. At that point in the worship I usually explain that I do not do those and then go on to engage with them in some form of remembered Bible chaos. Sometimes I get invited back.

In some ways it might seem more difficult to introduce remembered

Bibles to children who may not have heard so many Bible stories as adults, and therefore may have less to remember. The following conversation with Hannah,[13] then aged 7 years, shows what can happen:

Janet: We are going to remember the story of Jesus healing a blind person.

Hannah: I don't remember that one.

Janet: Well, what do you think happened first?

Hannah: There was a blind person?

Janet: OK – and what was happening? What did blind people do in those days?

Hannah: Nothing? The blind person was sitting by the road doing nothing.

Janet: So what happened next?

Hannah: Jesus came by.

Janet: And then ...

What this exchange shows is that children may actually be far more ready to take part than adults, who have decades of 'not talking in church' to inhibit their participation. Indeed, with the national literacy hour on the curriculum for most children, the idea of story-telling and the structure of a story is much more common currency for those under ten years of age than over. Here Lauren,[14] aged 6, tells her friend of the same age the story of the woman who anointed Jesus:

> *The woman had a bottle of perfume. And she poured it on Jesus's head while he was having his dinner. But he didn't mind. He said she did it 'cos she loved him.*

A few weeks later, Lauren reminded us that our community work was an example of 'how we love Jesus'.

All of the methods[15] described here have been used in mixed-age groups and there has been no evidence to suggest that children are less able to participate than group members of any other age. Usually, when small groups are used for informal remembering, each one will contain some children. Occasionally it will happen that most of the children fall into one group. Again, see this as an opportunity rather than a problem.

Baptism provides an ideal opportunity for remembering together, as we often begin with the story of Jesus's baptism. Baptismal candidates might be encouraged to develop their own remembered version of the story. Here's a version by Lauren, aged 7,[16] which shows how the remembering process can also be very imaginative. In addition, Lauren's 'punch line' about Jesus being astonished is a valuable insight.

When Jesus was baptised he was baptised in a river. All of his family were there. Some ducks, sheep on the hillside, horses to ride on. A man called John baptised him. Jesus might have been wearing a blue cloak and a green belt. His mum and dad were very excited. The three wise men were there as well. A loud voice said, 'You are my son,' which was God, and maybe Jesus was astonished.

Here are some examples of remembered gospel stories told by children that reveal similarly valuable interpretations.

Zaccheus was having one of those days (so began nine-year-old Gemma[17]) *and Jesus said to him, 'Do you mind not robbing all the people,' and he said, 'I don't mind,' and he came down from the tree and Jesus went home and had dinner with him and his family.*

Whilst some might say that Gemma's version omits the 'important' confessional aspect of the one Luke wrote, I like it. From time to time, we all have 'one of those days' – a sort of day for sitting in trees and waiting for Jesus to come by. There will be opportunities to remember this story again and add different details.

Moving on to the feeding of the five thousand, Gemma said:

And this boy said to Jesus, 'Would you mind sharing out this food?' and Jesus said, 'Yes,' and he shared out the bread and fish and everyone had a lot and all the leftovers went in baskets.

Another nine-year-old saw the child's contribution similarly:

He said to Jesus, 'I don't know if there will be enough.'

Both of these story-tellers felt that the child's role was more proactive, initiating and verbal than John's written version suggests. It illustrates the way in which children are the proactive theologians of the community, and long may that continue.

Nicole (aged 8 years [18]), who had linked her version of the baptism of Jesus to remembering her own baptism a year earlier, finished it with this affirmation: 'And God's voice said, "I'm proud of you."' This affirmation is one of the gifts people of all ages can discover in the remembered Bible process.

Hopefully what children get out of using this method is:

- an affirmation of their contribution and their right to participate in what happens in church as equals with adults;
- a fun time of sharing and chaos that is lively and memorable rather than tedious and boring, going above their heads and leaving them out.

What about the rest of the Bible?

So far this section has concentrated on remembering the life of Jesus. Yet there is much more to the Christian scriptures than that. Maybe you think some other parts of the Bible are more memorable. It is possible to use any bits of the Bible with these techniques. If I have concentrated on developing this method through the gospels, that is because it seemed easier and more relevant in the groups I was working with. Other parts of the Bible have been used for remembered versions, particularly in smaller groups. At the beginning of a meeting, for example, I might ask people what their most memorable text is and why. There are various texts from other parts of the Bible people do often remember: Psalm 23, the ten commandments (or at least some of them), as well as stories like Noah and the flood, the garden of Eden, Ruth, and so on. The method chosen to start off the remembering process will depend on how well known the 'bit' to be remembered seems to be. It may be a good idea to develop some idea of what people have in their remembered Bibles. 'Desert Island Bibles' is a game for doing that.

Desert Island Bibles

The idea behind Desert Island Bibles comes from a long-running BBC radio programme called *Desert Island Discs*. On this programme a well-known person is invited to choose eight records to take to a desert island. On the desert island the person is also allowed two books: the

Bible and the complete works of Shakespeare. Of the eight records to make it to the island with the survivor, seven are eventually washed away and only one is left. So what if most of the Bible is also washed away? What eight bits of the Bible would you want to keep and why? Ask the group to do this selection task individually and then either

- work in pairs and see what they have in common, gradually working in larger groups to see what are the most commonly chosen passages,

or

- if the group is not too big and you want to collect the whole 'canon' of remembered scripture for this group, then go through the Bible from its remembered beginning and see what people would have chosen as you go along.

People may refer to their remembered versions in a number of ways: by reference to the name of a book in the written version of the Bible, by a retelling of a part of the story, or by reference to a key character or event in the story. You may want to conclude with a time of telling some of the most frequently chosen excerpts as a way of introducing participants to the idea of telling their remembered versions to each other.

Ruth's relatives

The story of Ruth can be used as the basis for a remembered Bible study. It is a good one to choose when working in a multicultural context. Split the group up into at least three smaller groups, with, if possible, four people in each group. There is no need to be completely inflexible about this but the idea is to get each of the three groups to remember the beginning, middle or end of the story, and each person in the group to reflect on what is remembered through the eyes of one of the four main characters. It is quite reasonable to have more people in each group as 'crowd' or 'other relatives' for example.

The written version of the story of Ruth runs to several chapters and breaking it down into beginning, middle and end is as arbitrary as the chapter divisions in the written version might seem to be. Sometimes the middle will overlap with the beginning and/or the end but this is not important. Once you have a remembered beginning, middle and end, get the three groups together again and listen to the remembered story all the way through, with each group in turn telling their remembered part of it.

For the second stage, invite the participants to go back to their group and this time reflect on their part of the remembered story through the eyes of one of the four main characters: Naomi, Orpah, Boaz and Ruth. Bearing in mind that only Naomi and Ruth get a mention throughout the written version it will be interesting to see how the groups handle the absence or the silence of Orpah and Boaz at different points in the story. However, both may take the opportunity to acknowledge that there is more to everyone's story than just the bits in which they are present or in which they speak. Ruth had a story before she met Boaz and this aspect of her independent voice is something that many cultures still overlook for women. Orpah made a choice in difficult circumstances that meant she is silent later in the story. You may want to conclude your discussions with a series of short monologues like those given on page 97.

What next?

So now you are hooked on remembered versions of the Bible. You have been doing it as a group for some time, maybe a couple of years, at least once a month or more. You are surprised at what has happened:

- people talk more in worship;
- there is more life in the time spent together;
- people listen to each other more;
- interpretations of the Bible are shared more readily;
- it is enjoyable and fun too!

But if you wonder how this could be developed so that more growth might happen, here are a few ideas:

- take some photos of remembering sessions and display them where everyone can see them; invite participants to add their own captions;
- take a video of remembering sessions and use this or bits of it in subsequent sessions, or lend them to people who want to know more about it; *(Note: it may be necessary to get participants to sign a form allowing further use of this material.)*

- use remembering on other worship occasions: at baptism, at communion, at a funeral;
- use remembering at other times, for example to recall the story of a project, a journey or other shared activity;
- as a launch-pad for a new shared activity like making a quilt or collage based on the remembering, planning a journey based on the remembering, vision-building for a new piece of work.
- Go outside! Leave the cosy, warm space in which you usually operate for worship and education and try doing some remembered Bible stories in the fresh air. Think about your locality and see what it suggests for open-air remembering of Bible stories. Try doing the transfiguration up a hill, the stories of the fishermen by a lake or at the seaside, the crowd scenes in the street somewhere. You may need to make some plans in advance but street theatre can be popular and fun.

Remember to spend some time encouraging other people to take the role of facilitator so that the process can grow.

'Remembering the Bible' is not just fun or a way of making the Bible interesting. It is a way of doing Christian education that aims to challenge the very situations in which it is being remembered. In his literacy programme amongst Brazilian peasants, Paulo Freire set out an important educational method. According to his pedagogy it was no longer considered sufficient to educate 'the poor'. Rather, the very aims of education itself were exposed and reassembled. People didn't learn to read because what they read was not relevant to them. Literacy had become 'an act of knowledge' in which text and context were united in order to pose the simple, yet provocative, question: 'What is the relation between literacy, liberation and learning?' [19] The key thing about community education for Freire was that learning to read in a way relevant to their circumstances could give people a means with which to challenge the oppressive situation that had kept them illiterate for so long. Others have said that this kind of Freirian pedagogy takes place whenever educators continue a dialogue between texts and contexts, providing similar opportunities to challenge and change unfair situations. The method of remembering the Bible that I have described is like this. For the method described here, the text was the Bible, while the context was life on the edge in urban Britain. People who were not very confident in reading the Bible could use an oral method to question the very situations in which they found themselves. It was in this Freirian tradition that the 'remembering the Bible' strategy described here operated.

The two important ingredients are present: oppression and an absence of literacy. There are several obvious kinds of oppression operating in the context that has been described. The first is one of poverty. Most of this work was done in some of the poorest urban parts of the UK. Even in Western Europe this material poverty is accompanied by many kinds of social poverty of which education is an obvious one, hence the add-on absence of literacy. But there are other oppressions. There are often silences amongst adults in churches – a combined effect of years of poverty, classism, racism, sexism and poor education, including the eventual outcome of ineffectual Christian education which has clearly not been liberating. In itself this Christian education is partly the product of the retreat of biblical scholarship from the faith community to the academy. In removing themselves to the academy, biblical scholars have ceased to engage with the people or the issues of the contemporary faith context. Furthermore, most 'biblical critics' have been slow to 'read against the grain' of the Bible, or to question the status quo and generally-held suppositions. Rather they have been largely content to re-enact the ideologies and power relations that exist around them. What is required is for 'socially engaged' biblical scholars to recommit themselves to similar situations using methods relevant to these contexts.[20]

For those faith communities living on the edge, what is needed is a pedagogy that can engage with both oppression and literacy. From my earlier work with people with communication difficulties came the idea of using not written but remembered versions. From the work with others in marginalised communities came the idea of putting the Bible back in their hands as a tool for engaging with oppression. It was Herzog who linked the pedagogic work of Freire and Jesus, pointing out that they both worked with the poor and oppressed and with peasants, and comparing the imperial or colonialist situations in first-century Palestine and twentieth-century Brazil. He went on to affirm that 'both Jesus and Freire knew the power of what we call religion to liberate and oppress'. It was obvious to Herzog that Freire, in his visual culture, would use pictures and literacy as his tools, and that Jesus, from an oral culture, would use story-telling. From here it is not very far to suggest that, in a not-highly-literate culture, remembered stories might be used as the basis of a curriculum that would work with the liberating side of religion to be 'world-shaking' rather than 'world-maintaining'. [21]

This contrast probably underlies some of the reasons why not every Christian faith community would want to use 'remembered texts'. The tensions between maintaining and shaking the world of the church or the wider community exist in all of the faith communities with which I have worked. In some, one will dominate the group's ethos and practice; in others, the other. Where 'world-maintaining' is the dominant ethos and practice of the group, then a method and curriculum that is in essence 'world-shaking' will at best take longer to develop or at worst be rejected outright.

The question of 'What happens next?' is a real one. Even after using these methods for more than five years the process was not necessarily complete. New circumstances challenge and change the way the methods are used over time: the people in the group, the group facilitator/s, what is happening in the local community. Recording some of the occasions when we have used remembered texts together allowed us to review them, and discuss what was happening further. A visual display of groups using the methods will allow others to view what went on and determine if they would want to use them.

'Critical pedagogy' has been defined as 'opening up institutional spaces for marginalised students to give voice to their experience and to develop a critical analysis of oppressive social systems in order to transform them in accordance with their interests.' [22] Whilst it is important to be aware of the shortcomings of the process described here, using remembered texts has led to the opening up of institutional space, in this case the worship and learning space of the faith community. This method has enabled marginalised participants to give voice to their experiences as a first stage in analysing the prevailing social system and its transformation.

NOTES

[1] Lorraine Beal has been a volunteer at the Shiregreen URC Children and Families Project (quotation used with permission).

[2] Members of Pitsmoor Methodist Church, St James URC and Shiregreen URC from the Sheffield Inner City Ecumenical Mission, from group work in 2000.

[3] From a discussion with Shiregreen URC on 03.07.05.

4   Jennifer Taylor, aged 8, is a member of Shiregreen URC (quotation used with permission).

5   Thanks to Peter Smithies, a member of Shiregreen URC, for this suggestion and for the illustration (used with permission).

6   'Halle-halle-halle-lu-u-jah', a song originating in the Caribbean, can be found in *Many and Great* (Wild Goose Publications 1990).

7   These examples from a list generated at St James URC on 23rd September 2001

8   Some of this material previously appeared in a paper prepared for the journal *Semeia*.

9   They were first used in this form at the East Midlands Synod (URC) Mission School, May 2000, and have been refined by use in other places since.

10 We used the video of the film *Sister Act*, starring Whoopi Goldberg, as an introduction to mission on the edge of the church.

11 I was once told 'We can't do this. We've got a minister.' The implication here was that the style of leadership was the stumbling block.

12 I accept that it is difficult to read specific impairments back into the biblical text and that some people will refer to this story as 'the boy with the evil spirit'. As I know more children with epilepsy than with evil spirits I use the title given here.

13 Hannah Warwicker is a member of Shiregreen United Reformed Church (quotation used by permission).

14 Lauren Wigfield is a member of Shiregreen United Reformed church (quotation used with permission).

15 This includes the liturgy and stories in the later sections of the book. All of this stuff is meant for real all-age worship where children and adults are not separated but try to worship and learn together all of the time.

16 Lauren Tackeray is a member of Shiregreen United Reformed Church (quotation used with permission).

17 Gemma Hague was a member of the 5th Sheffield Girls' Brigade Company (quotation used with permission).

18 Nicole Smith was a member of the 5th Sheffield Girls' Brigade Company (quotation used by permission).

19 Pages 31 and 33 of P.V. Taylor (1993).

20 G.O. West (1999)

21 Pages 25–28 of W. R. Herzog (1994).

22 A. Kramer-Dahl, (1995) page 242.

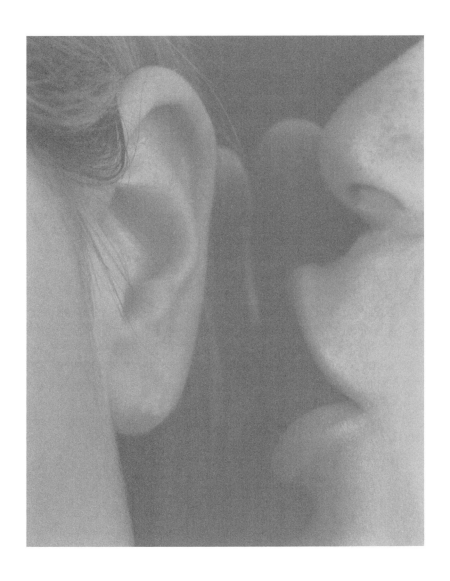

Chapter two

Reflecting on remembered Bibles

1. Remembering the Bible at Christmas

A good time of year to include remembered versions of the Bible in other ways is Christmas. The story is pretty well known, and often 'told' in a hybridised form anyway. There are plenty of different sorts of illustrations that can be used. A 'Remember that Nativity' requires no previous rehearsal, just people willing to turn up, choose their role/s and take part. Everyone can participate because the members of the group not acting particular characters can provide the narrative. You may find that particularly memorable words and phrases survive the remembering. Alternatively, Christmas can provide an ideal opportunity for more creative and imaginative rememberings. An example of this is a quiz format for 'Remembering the Bible at Christmas'.

TV quiz shows have become very popular in our culture. They are now available as gifts in various forms and highly rated episodes are shown at peak times. All this is a stark contrast to much of what the church offers at Christmas. So why not swap formats and go for the wacky idea of a quiz show on remembering the Bible at Christmas. For those who want the *Millionaire* version, chocolate money (fair trade of course) can be shared out at the end.

Aims:

- To connect remembered and written versions of the Nativity narrative;
- To unscramble the version of the Nativity used in most plays etc at Christmas, and find out who wrote what;
- To have fun!

What you will need:

- 4 sheets of brightly coloured paper, poster-sized;
- sticky tape or glue stick;
- smaller strips of paper.

On the four poster-sized sheets put the headings, one on each sheet, of the names attributed to the four gospel writers: 'Matthew', 'Mark', 'Luke' and 'John'.

On the smaller strips of paper, write a 'clue' from the Nativity narrative such as:

- shepherds in the fields
- a long list of ancestors
- Quirinius, Governor of Syria
- wise men follow a star
- the Word made flesh
- a stable and a manger
- gold, frankincense and myrrh
- Mary sings a song
- Mary visits her cousin Elizabeth
- Herod, the king of Judea
- an angel speaks to Mary
- an angel speaks to Joseph
- a chorus of angels
- a man named John

You may add others. You may also want to add some who are not in the written accounts but often appear in remembered or fictionalised accounts: innkeepers for example.

What to do

The game may proceed in a number of different ways. Crucial to the remembered method is collaboration. This is not really about finding an overall winner. Put up the posters and give out the clues. Make sure the clues are shared between at least two people, but in some places a group or a row (those pews again) or a family might share a clue. You may want to give a few more verbal clues before the game begins:

- one writer says nothing about the Nativity;
- one has it in a different form to the other two;
- the story we usually tell is a combination of what was written by two others, but they didn't write the same things.

Give the participants a chance to discuss their clue and even the clues of those around them. Who do they think wrote about the clue they have? What other clues does their clue go with?

Invite participants to offer ideas about which clues they think go with which writer. Where people have difficulty deciding, include more people to help, have a vote, phone a friend, but most of all, try not to make individuals look foolish. Stick the clues on the poster of the written gospel in which they appear.

At the end summarise what has been shared and ask for comments on what was surprising or unexpected.

2. MAUNDY THURSDAY

Using remembered versions of the Bible can also influence the way it is used at other times in worship. Here is an example of a short drama for a Maundy Thursday evening service that has features relevant to the remembered way of using the Bible together:

- it includes all ages together; the drama can have participants of almost any age;
- it builds on the common shared experiences; in this case it is based around the experience of running a community project together and the meetings that are involved in this;
- it includes bits of the Bible which have been remembered and worked with during the year: amongst these are references to feeding the five thousand, healing Peter's mother-in-law, visiting Martha and Mary, and the Holy Week narrative itself;
- it includes some of the background to studying the Bible, for example its gender bias;
- it shares features with common culture, in this case the television 'sitcom' genre, which is familiar in our context.

For this sketch you will need at least ten people, of any age or gender. There are four disciples (D1-4), Jesus (J), Martha (M), Peter (P), Judas, Thomas and Mary (she does not speak). You can, if you want, add more non-speakers or split the parts for the four disciples up further to give more people speaking parts.

The Last Supper

D1:   Is this the meeting of the Disciples of Jesus Executive Committee?

D2:   Yes it is and you're late.

D1:   I'm sorry, it's my first meeting.

D2:   It'll be your last if you don't buck up.

J: Right, well let's get this show on the road. Appointment of officers for this meeting? Peter, you take the minutes; Martha, you make the tea. Second item, minutes of the last meeting, held at Martha's house – any comments?

M: Yes, I don't see a record here of what I actually said. Peter seems to have left it out. I said 'You are the Christ, the Messiah,' but he hasn't put that.

J: Yes, Peter, why did you leave that out?

P: *(mumbling)* Women! I knew we shouldn't have had any on this committee. *(Corrects paper)*

D3:   I see Mary's here again. Why does she come? She never says anything.

D4:   I know what you mean. You'd have thought she'd have stayed away after the scene she made at that meeting at Simon's house when she poured all that perfume over the Chair.

J: All right you two, that will do. If some of the verbal people here thought as much about what they said as Mary thinks about what she doesn't say, we'd get along a lot better. Item three, a report from the catering subcommittee. Peter, wasn't your mother-in-law going to present that. She doesn't seem to be here.

P: Well she's got a headache so she's stayed at home. *(Mumbles)* Best place for her if you ask me.

J: Martha, are you going to present that item then?

M: Yes, I could do if you like. We just wanted to say, it's getting a bit difficult on the catering side when we don't know how many are going to turn up. I know you managed with those couple of fish and out of date bread cakes [1] that time, but with a bit more organisation we could do a nice spread.

J: Martha, Martha you are troubled by many things. How many times do I have to explain it to you all. Look, it's simple. *(Takes bread cake)* This is my body broken for you. *(Pause)* Got it? Now, can we crack on? I've got an appointment in the Garden of Gethsemane in an hour.

P: Could we take the financial report from Judas before he has to go? *(Murmurs of agreement from others)*

Judas: Well, there's not much to say. We're about thirty pieces of silver down on the month's end balance but I hope to have sorted that out by the end of the evening.

J: Yes, I know you have to leave early, Judas. Could you try to leave

quietly please? Hope to catch you later. Now where had we got
to? *(Judas leaves)*

M: I think that brings us to the date of the next meeting. That should
be Joseph's house on Sunday evening I think.

J: Well, I'll not be there. In fact *(takes cup)* I'll not drink of the fruit
of the vine again until I drink it in my Father's kingdom.

P: Not be there? But what do you mean. You're always there. You said
where two or three are gathered together you'd always be there.
We can't have a meeting without you. *(Murmurs of agreement)*

J: Yes, well, I was going to say something about that, Peter. Do you
ever think we might be getting a bit bogged down with meetings?

D1: Bogged down?

D2: With meetings?

All: We don't know what you mean.

J: I see. Well, perhaps I could arrive a bit late.

Thom: A bit late! But you know we always lock the door when the meeting starts so no one can interrupt us. So if you're going to turn up
late, how will we recognise you?

All: *(turning towards Jesus)* Yes, how will we recognise you?[2]

3. WERE YOU THERE?

Were you there when they crucified my Lord?[3]
This activity can be used any time between Holy Week and Pentecost. It
invites participants to identify with the events of Jesus's passion and
resurrection through the eyes of the people recorded in the gospels as
having been there, and some others as well. From the end of the gospels
to the beginning of the book of Acts there are several occasions when
groups of Jesus's followers are found together either going over some
recent events or waiting. It is these gatherings that are the starting point
for this activity.

Decide which part of the Easter story you are going to revisit
together. Assemble a list of people invited to be present and to be
remembered. You may want to do this in advance so participants get a
chance to think about who they will be remembering. You may want to
do it in small groups so that people work together on remembering one
or more characters, or you may want to 'just go for it'.

A list of participants might include well-remembered ones like

- Thomas
- Peter
- Mary, the mother of Jesus,
- Mary of Bethany,

as well as some less well remembered like
- Matthias
- Joseph of Arimathea
- Joanna
- Salome

or even some anonymous ones like
- The Syro-Phoenician woman,
- A healed leper
- Jairus's daughter

Whatever you choose, keep in mind that it is probably much easier to work with remembering a character like Peter, who is well known in the gospels, than one like Joanna, who is only referred to in passing. Furthermore, try not to get stuck into stereotypes. It is not necessary for men always to remember men and women only to remember women. Nor is it necessary to completely ignore the contribution of those under 12 years of age. A girl child might bring new insights to the role of Peter; an older man could present Mary of Magdala in a new way. Try not always to give the part of Peter to the alpha-male in the group, or Mary of Magdala to the most outspoken woman. Whilst it might seem that a quieter person would prefer a role like Joanna or even an anonymous part, so that they do not need to say much, equally it could be more interesting to have Peter played by such a person, so that we hear some different voices and different stories for a change.

If the event is to represent a meeting of the discipleship group, either pre- or post-Easter, then consider serving food or drink to make it more informal. Dressing up is another option. The idea is then to remember what you can, and imagine the rest. Using information and ideas gathered from around the edges of the gospel, it is possible to weave a story for any of the characters. This can be done by individuals, or by small groups working together to remember the same character. It gives people a chance to offer their interpretation of the Easter events and to discover 'Were you there?'

4. Jesus's lifeline

This is a good activity for the end of the liturgical year when you might want to subvert the order of such things with a bit of creative chaos. It goes well on the Feast of Christ the King (Last Sunday after Pentecost). The aim of the activity is to provide a way of collecting together the things people have remembered about Jesus's life. It can also provide a good introduction to the remembered Bible method, in which case it can be referred to as 'assembling the contents page of our remembered gospel'.

What you will need:

- a very, very, very long piece of string – enough to stretch across the widest part of the space you are using, or down the middle;
- a lot of clothes pegs, at least enough for each member of the group to have one.

What to do

Explain that the string represents Jesus's life. Have someone hold one end of the string, explaining that this end is his birth. Have someone else hold the other end of the string and explain that this end is his death, resurrection and ascension. In case there are any members of the group who want to argue that Jesus existed before he was born or has an existence in the Godhead now, makes sure the piece of string is long enough for both people to hold a bit of spare. This saves long, time-consuming, and invariably fruitless, theological arguments.

Invite the group each to take a peg and to peg it on the string at the place they think their example happened in Jesus's life, saying what it represents. Thus up at the 'birth' end of the string you should have things like conception, birth in Bethlehem, growing up in Nazareth, visit to the temple as a boy, etc. At the 'death' end of the string you should have the events of Holy Week and the fifty glorious days after the resurrection.

In the middle you might have all sorts of things. For example, someone might say 'When he was a young man he cured a blind person. I think he was about twenty so I'll put it there,' placing the peg in the middle of the string. See this as an opportunity rather than a mistake. It should be considered alongside such apocryphal tales as 'the healing of Andrew's mother-in-law' (Who says he didn't have one?), or the healing of the twelve lepers (or whatever memorable number seems to have come to mind) or 'the time Jesus knocked on the doors of the houses and told people to go out and tell others about him'. All of these examples have really happened in groups doing this activity.

Carry on putting pegs on the string until everyone who wants to has had a go, or you run out of pegs. Some contributions may be duplicates. This doesn't matter either. It does help you to build up a picture of what bits of the gospels people have found the most memorable. In a group of mixed abilities it's useful to encourage people to work together so that everyone can take part.

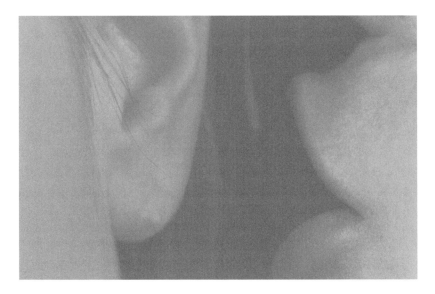

NOTES

1 Bread cakes are what you call bread rolls in Sheffield.
2 First appeared in J Lees (2001) 'Remembering the Bible in Worship' in Rowland and Vincent (eds) *Bible and Practice*. Sheffield: Urban Theology Unit, pages 41–43.
3 The first line of what is described as an American Folk Hymn, *Rejoice and Sing* 227. Oxford University Press, 1991.

Part two

From the edge of the Bible

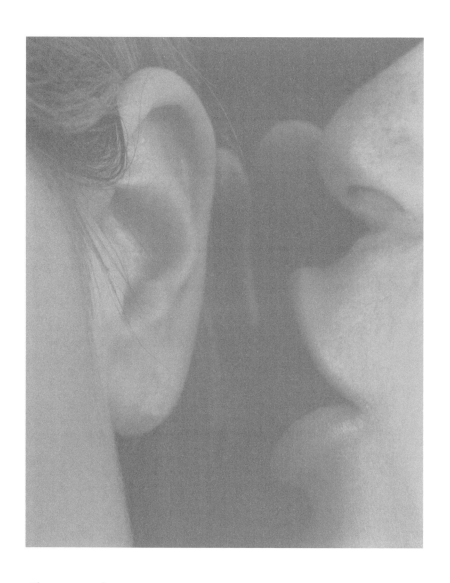

Chapter three

Playing with parables

The church is losing its attractiveness. Fewer and fewer people seem to be drawn to some of the ways we now have of being church. In considering how we might make the church more winsome - more attractive - the way we use the Bible has a part to play. Maybe it is not very winsome to everyone of different ages and abilities to expect them to listen to long extracts from the Bible or to read to them from such a huge book if they cannot do that very readily themselves. Another way of understanding *'winsome'* is in the phrase *'you win some and you lose some'*. By this I mean that some people are attracted by what they experience of the more chaotic church of the remembered Bible and some are repelled. It seems to me that this is very true to the experiences of Jesus's ministry. Some were attracted to it and some were quite definitely repelled. One of the devices Jesus used in his ministry that attracted and repelled people was teaching in parables. On the whole, in *dead churches* parables have become used in such hackneyed and predictable ways that they no longer do this. In *chaotic edge churches* one of the things we might do is rediscover the ways in which parables can be winsome - or not.

Using parables

Jesus told parables about real life in order that people might understand it better: see oppression, injustice, fairness, inequality, power struggles and so on that were going on round them and act to bring about change. Jesus used parables to uncover things that were right in front of people but which they had not noticed. Thus they were supposed to include an element of surprise. If there was not a realisation - 'Ah, now I get it!' - then there was no point in telling the parable. Jesus did not tell parables about the church (it did not exist!) or to be 'nice'.

There are two main ways in which I want to explore the use of parables. In the first method, we look behind the parable at its social setting in first-century Palestine, as far as this is possible. This is the approach of Herzog (1994). [1] We look to see what social conditions, economic situation, gender roles, power struggles from the first century Jesus was trying to deconstruct. Then we understand what it was/is about real life and the struggle for fullness of life that Jesus was on about. Next we try to find a way of tackling the same thing in our own context. We need to see what the contrasts within the original parable were: for example, between good shepherds and hired hands, between landowners and stewards, between landowners and workers, between a rich person and a poor person, between a judge and a peasant woman. Then we have to find parallels in our context: between managers and workers, between women and men, between rich nations and poor nations.

In his book *Parables as Subversive Speech*, William Herzog calls the parable of the talents found in Matthew's gospel 'The Whistle Blower'. By closer consideration of the structure of the household in the ancient world, Herzog is able to show that this is the context of the parable about the master and the three servants. In our churchy way we have wrongly identified the master with God and tried to make the parable into a story about obedience in the Christian life, when it is really about corruption in the household. Later in this chapter there are two different examples of a contemporary reworking of the parable of the whistle blower.

It is followed by two versions of the parable of the sower, one rural and one urban. Although this has long been one of my favourite parables, especially for acting out, I have never been satisfied with the interpretation offered in the written gospels. These are clearly a spiritualised allegory, even though they are offered up as Jesus's own words. Whilst I have been happy to use the story in this way with an emphasis on personal growth, I have hankered after a more 'Herzog-esque' interpretation.

According to Herzog, the story has to be comprehensible in its real, original context: agricultural practice in first-century Palestine, a Jewish state under Roman occupation. In that time most peasants would have worked the land for some landowner. Thus the sower of our story is probably not the landowner, but a tenant or worker. It is of little or no interest to him (were there any female sowers?) if the yield is high or not. That is only of interest to the landowner who would be concerned about making a profit on the land.

We have to go to the edges of the field if we are to find Jesus's original interpretation. The edges of the field, according to the story, are the sites of greater interest and activity, even if it is harder for things to grow there. This makes sense in the light of Jewish law and tradition that the edges of the field should be left to be gleaned by the poor, the widows and orphans. Remember Ruth who gleans the edges of Boaz's fields like this. The sower is currently employed by the landowner but could well be out of work tomorrow, next week or next season. The route to the margins of society was never very far away for a peasant.

For those on the margins of that society, what grew or did not grow at the edges of the field was of great interest and Jesus knew this. He is, in effect, saying to his audience of edge-dwellers, 'This bit of the field is yours, so pay attention.' We learn that things do not grow well at the edges of fields: birds eat the seeds where the ground is hard, or weeds compete for light and moisture with what has been sown. In some rocky places it is just too hard for crops to grow. So what will the poor get from the edges of the field? Not much to live on by the sounds of it. That is unless the landowner is more generous, like Boaz who fancied Ruth enough to give the reapers instructions to leave her a bit extra. [2]

So now the story goes like this:

> *Listen here you lot. Some of you have worked for landowners and you know about sowing crops. You know where the plants will grow best: in the middle of the field. That's obvious, but you have no access to that crop. You know it won't grow very well at the edges. Won't the birds eat what doesn't germinate when it falls on the hard-baked ground of the footpath? Won't the weeds compete for soil and moisture? In some places won't it be just too rocky for plants to grow? So what are the poor, the widows and the orphans supposed to live on if all they are allowed is what grows around the edges of the fields? No one can stay alive on that. It takes an honest and generous landowner to make a share of the best grain available to the poor. If you have a brain then use it.*

It is just possible that a knowing sower could swing the balance the way of the marginalised a bit by sending a little more seed to the edges of the field – but maybe that is a different story.

Having got to know the sower in this way, now we need to transplant the story into the twenty-first century and see what sense it makes there. Here there are plenty of edges to attend to. Questions about who gets what at the edges, and whether or not it is enough to live on, are still pertinent, but urban and rural contexts may demand different settings, hence the two versions of the story later in the chapter.

A mirror to the church

The other method I like to use is to expose the way the parables have been used (over-used and sanitised) by the church. This way we can hold a mirror up to the church in which it can see itself through the parable.

Most parables have been allegorised to include interpretations of the main characters as God, Jesus, the church, the world, etc. Having looked at the first method, we can see that this is not what Jesus originally intended, but it has become common currency in the church. Jesus did not tell parables about ministry, hymn-singing, flower rotas, friendship. But often we have taken the sting out of the parable by recasting and re-emphasising these imposed, safer themes. But, rather than completely throw this out, we can use it to say, 'This is the parable the church is expecting, but look at it in this mirror and see something else about yourselves.'

A key point about using parables in this way is that we need to be particularly alert to the shortcomings of the traditional interpretation by the church. The characters and experiences we will choose for mirror parables will highlight a challenge to the church's interpretation. If the church thinks the parable of the Good Shepherd is about being a good minister (it is not; it is about managing priorities), ours will be about being a good enough minister. If the church thinks the parable of the Good Samaritan is about being friendly (it is not; it is about insiders and outsiders) we will ask what exactly is a good friend. Of course, this also allows us to make up parables about the church – like a parable of the church as a badly maintained house, or ones in which people argue about the furniture or the flower rota. These are not irrelevant but reflect something of what the church has in some places been reduced to by its neglect of the winsome nature of the gospel. We need to wake people up to this deathly behaviour. Parables can help us do that.

Other ways of 'getting into parables'

You can use the remembered method with parables. This can be combined with some 'hands on' things to do: here are some ideas.

'Hands on'
For the parable of the mustard seed you need mustard seeds. Participants should each have one in their hand. This proves more memorable than a thousand words on the subject. As Rebecca, aged 7 3, says (holding a mustard seed), 'Oh, yeah, this is the one about the very little tiny seed that grows up into a great big tree and it grows and grows and all the birds go and live there.' Exactly.

You may be, as I was, a bit sceptical about such a small seed growing into a tree. Here is a conversation about that with Reece, aged 9 years [4]:

Janet: Could such a small seed really grow into a tree though?

Reece: It could. It could if you left it for a while. If you left it for two
           years or more, then it could grow into a tree.

With these words Reece expressed why it had been better to use the
remembered Bibles strategy for a longer (then four years) rather than
shorter (initially six months) time.

There are other parables that benefit from 'hands on'. If dealing with
the parable of the yeast, get some, and some flour, and mix them up and
wait and see what happens. If you work with a group that has a fixed
time limit on worship, then do this near the beginning and use warm
water. Better still, let everyone have some and do it together. Rather
than 'here's some I made earlier', you can all eat the fruits of your
labours later.

Charades can work well with the shorter parables. This has already
been described for the parable of the sower in the first chapter of the
book (page 24)

Using the language of parables

The language of parables is subversive. Both the images and the way they
play on words can be used to challenge in other settings. Prayers, new
parables, reflections and so on can all include parable images or
language.

The whole purpose of parables is to bring us to the moment when we
see the point – newly, clearly, with a sense of challenge. It is not about
rehearsing some tired old message that has lost its punch. For some
people the methods of using parables described here will be attractive or
winsome. They will be stimulated, find encouragement, laugh, stretch
themselves in these interpretations. Others will find them repellent. They
will reject the idea that parables can be interpreted this way, and will
become defensive, angry and blustering. But that is what parables are
supposed to do. They are about choosing or rejecting the way Jesus
demonstrates. They are not about telling nice stories. In this way, through
the use of parables, you will find 'you win some and you lose some'.

Parable-telling Christ,
the life you show us goes beyond
the death that surrounds us.
Help us to move the furniture and the world;
to sing new songs and embrace new opportunities;
to take risks with and for the gospel.

1. The bad burger bar owner[5]

There was once a man who owned three burger bars in a poor part of the city. He was a self-made man and proud of it. He'd started from scratch and worked long hours, expecting others who worked for him to do the same.

One day he decided that he had worked hard enough and he'd have a long holiday; take his wife to see their family in Australia. Before he went he appointed three managers for the three burger bars. He called them together and said: 'Now look here, I'm leaving these burger bars for you to manage while I'm away. I want you to do a good job, as if I was managing them myself. When I get back I expect those burger bars to be running just like they are now, and if not then I'll have something to say about it.' And he left.

While he was away the three managers managed the burger bars. The first was much like the owner except worse. He realised that if he was to show a profit when the owner returned and make a bit for himself, he'd have to be even more ruthless. He cut the wages of the staff and employed more staff without contracts. He even employed underage workers. Everyone was expected to work even longer hours and to serve customers even more quickly. People who went off sick from the stress were sacked without notice and, as he'd already got rid of the union representation and the Chaplain to Marginal Workers, they had no recourse.

The second manager was much the same and he too found ways around the law so that he could get as much as he could out of the burger bar. He bought in cheap meat, and some wondered if it was fit for human consumption. He used genetically modified ingredients and didn't declare it. But once again the workers had no recourse to justice.

The third manager was shocked by what he found when he took up the job and gradually it dawned on him that only he could do something about the unjust situation in the burger bar. He called in the Chaplain for Marginal Workers and asked for help in respect of the minimum wage regulations, maternity pay and the like. He got an environmental health officer down to the burger bar and began to improve the facilities. The workers were a bit wary of him and still thought he might betray them to the owner, so they didn't really trust him, although absenteeism did go down a bit and people agreed they preferred working there in the new conditions.

Then the owner came back from his holiday.

He called the managers together and asked them how the burger business was going.

The first manager said: 'You asked me to manage a burger bar which was making £500 a week profit. Well, I've doubled your profit. It's now making £1000 a week.'

'Well done,' said the owner. 'You're a good manager – you can work for me again!'

The second manager said: 'You asked me to manage a burger bar which was making £200 a week profit. Look, it's now making £400!'

'Well done,' said the owner. 'You're also a good manager and can work for me again.'

The third manager came and said, 'I know you're a hard man but I was appalled at what I found at that burger bar. Workers' rights being disregarded. Health and safety standards ignored. It was dreadful and needed putting right. I've tried to make some improvements and as a result you're lucky that we're still breaking even.'

The owner was angry with the third manager and called him an interfering twit, and who did he think he was making all these decisions without authority from him, and a bit of hard work never hurt anyone and so on.

He dismissed him there and then, saying: 'Now you're unemployed too, with no reference from me, what kind of job do you think you'll get? You'll be on the dole – serves you right.'

Now the third manager had a home and family to support and he realised things would be grim. He wondered what kind of reception he'd get at the job centre, and if any of the burger bar workers would speak up for him if he took his case to an industrial tribunal for unfair dismissal.

The workers at the third burger bar were puzzled about what had happened to the manager. They began to talk amongst themselves, quietly of course so as not to raise suspicion. They had never liked the owner but they were afraid to cross him. Should they support the third manager at the industrial tribunal or not?

One of the workers who got maternity benefit because of what the manager had done said: 'We owe that manager a lot. He made our jobs bearable and helped us, and at considerable risk to himself.' And some of the others agreed, although some were wary.

If you have a mouth, then use it!

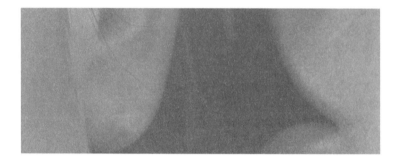

2. The college whistle blower [6]

There were three students about to start training for the ministry at a well-known theological college. On the first day the Principal met them and said: 'Work hard, keep your noses clean and you'll learn a lot from us because we're the place that really knows how to train people for ministry.' With that he disappeared into his office and they didn't see him again until the end of the course.

The first student looked around and saw students struggling to cope with the workload. But knowing that the Principal had said he must work hard he went into the college library and read all the books by the great men and wrote long essays on them all and their ideas, although they had little practical application. By the end of it he was near breakdown with little sleep and RSI but he had achieved 1,000 credits and was sure he could be a future college Principal.

The second student looked around and saw the outdated teaching methods and the unfair methods of assessment. But remembering that the Principal had said this place really knew how to train ministers he went into the computer suite (donated by a rich American benefactor) and looked lots of things up on the internet and copied this into his own work. By the end he was near breakdown with little sleep and RSI but he had achieved 500 credits and was sure he could be a future General Secretary.

The third student looked around and was appalled at what she found: in every year several students were unable to complete their courses, tutors failed to keep appointments with students, dates and times of lectures and seminars were changed at random and not communicated to anyone, students' work remained unread and unmarked. But she remembered that the Principal had said they were to keep their noses clean, so for a while she said nothing whilst struggling hard with the injustice of it all. Finally, at her wits' end, she tried several methods to get these and other injustices changed through various committees and the more sympathetic tutors. By the end she was completely broken, had had no sleep and had achieved 10 credits, and was sure she would never practise ministry again.

On the day of the annual prize-giving, the Principal came out of his office. He said to the first student: 'How have you been getting on with our excellent course?' and the student replied. 'Well, you told me to work hard and I did. I've read all the books in the library and written all these essays and gained 1,000 credits.' And the Principal was pleased with him and said: 'Well done, you good and hardworking student. Surely you will be a future college Principal.' And he gave him a first-class honours degree.

He asked the second student: 'How have you been getting on with our excellent course?' and the student replied, 'Well, I believed you really knew how to train ministers here so I've used your excellent computer facilities and I've written all these essays and I've gained 500 credits.' And the Principal was pleased with him and said: 'Well done, you resourceful and enterprising student. Surely you will be a future General Secretary.' And he gave him a second-class honours degree.

He came to the third student and asked her: 'How have you been getting on with our excellent course?' And the student, using the last ounce of strength and courage she had, and ungluing her tongue from the roof of her mouth, said, 'Your course is not excellent; students are really suffering. You say you are listening but I see little evidence of that. Appointments are not kept and work is not adequately marked. Students feel undermined and their experience is not valued, and in trying to get justice here I have only got 10 credits.'

'You worthless student,' said the Principal. 'Why couldn't you just keep your nose clean and your mouth shut like the rest of them? You don't deserve to qualify and you'll never get a job if I have anything to do with it. Take the 10 credits from her and give them to the one that has 1,000 and throw her out of college.'

Now, which one of the three students would be the one you would want working with you alongside marginalised and oppressed people?

If you have a mouth, then use it!

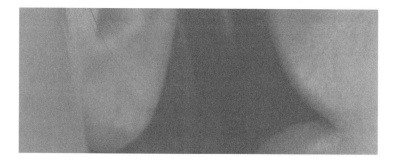

3. The farmer

There once was a farmer and, although he lived in a generally prosperous country with a congenial climate, farming had, over his lifetime, become an increasingly hard business. More and more of his companions were going out of business, or finding it hard just to get by: the suicide rate had soared and depression was endemic.

One springtime, as usual, he had to decide what to plant on his farm. What would give him the best yield? What would bring in the biggest profit? What would be best for the land? He struggled with these questions for some time.

First he approached a potato company. His ground was good for potatoes and many people grew potatoes in that area. The potato company said: 'Before you can grow potatoes for us, you must plough up all those footpaths. Footpaths are useless for growing potatoes. The ground is too hard and it's a waste of space. Besides which we don't want people walking all over our potatoes. And remember, if we agree to use your farm, you can only grow our potatoes, and sell them to us, and nothing else for the duration of this agreement.'

Secondly the farmer approached a wheat company. His ground was good for wheat and many people grew wheat in that area. The wheat company said: 'Before you can grow wheat for us, you must plough up all of those hedges. Hedges are useless for growing wheat, and they are particularly useless for harvesting with giant combine harvesters. And remember, if we agree to use your farm, you must take out a contract with 'Giant Combine Harvesters Ltd' with whom we have a contract, to use their machinery for the duration of this agreement.'

Thirdly the farmer approached a rape-seed company. His ground was good for rape-seed and many people grew rape-seed in that area. The rape-seed company said: 'Before you can grow rape-seed for us, you must move all of those big boulders. Boulders are useless for growing rape-seed, and they are particularly useless for planting it using extra-fast seed drills. And remember, if we agree to use your farm, you must also agree to let us use your land for trials of our genetically modified seeds for the duration of this agreement.'

The farmer went back to his farm and thought about it all. He did not want to plough up the footpaths, because he and his family and his neighbours and other people relied on them to get from place to place. He did not want to plough up his hedges, because if he did that where would the butterflies and birds and small mammals live? He did not want to move all the boulders, for where would the grass snakes, slow worms and beetles live if he did? He did not want to enter into any agreements that meant he could not choose what crops to grow or how to grow them, and where all the profits went to big companies far away.

So he went back to his land and began to walk the footpaths, and examine the hedges, and rest, from time to time, on a boulder or two. It was a lovely spring morning. The sun was warming everything, birds were beginning to nest in the hedges, flowers were starting to bloom and he even saw a grass snake slither under a rock. He met some people coming along a footpath and they had a friendly chat. All in all, it was clear this was a beautiful place: a treasure to be enjoyed and shared and cherished.

So he went back to the farmhouse and began to draw up plans for contacting the local environmental organisations to see if they could help him. It would be good to have more people visiting and seeing just how lovely it was. It would be good to have more native animals and plants. It would be risky. Maybe there were some seed crops that would be compatible with his vision. First of all, he would set aside the edges of the fields for the animals and plants and visitors to enjoy.

4. The regeneration workers [7]

Some regeneration workers started work in a city that was well known for its poverty. Social inclusion was the language of the day and everyone had grand ideas about how exclusion was going to be overcome by local and national initiatives. The regeneration workers had also caught this vision and went about the work with enthusiasm. There were many new grants available to help local groups. There were local strategic plans and local action plans. There were programmes for health, employment, training and childcare. Indeed the regeneration workers had briefcases brimming with things to offer the excluded local people.

At the first meeting the city council said, 'It will be too hard for them,' and the regeneration worker said, 'I'll do it for them,' but the local people just resented being patronised. At the second meeting a group with some experience in regeneration said, 'Give us the money and we'll make sure they get some of it,' but the local people were angry about the strategy and would not work with the larger group. At the third meeting a few local people who had come along quickly started to get keen and interested, but the deadline for the application was looming and, with not enough resources available, the application was not made in time. The local people felt betrayed, whilst the regeneration worker was burnt out by the workload. Meanwhile all around the edges of the city there were small groups of local excluded people, some in touch with regeneration workers and some who were not, who got on with the task themselves, little by little, of making sense of the grant system and getting local projects off the ground. None of these were large initiatives, and many did not last for more than a short time, but whilst they were there they gave life to some of the edge-dwelling people and offered some encouragement and hope in those places.

If you have a brain, then use it.

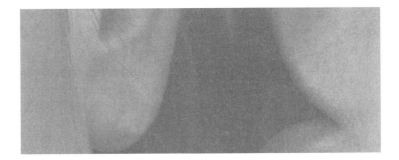

5. The good friend

There was once a person who set out as usual one morning to go to work by car. The car was in reasonable condition and the person was a good driver. However, the car was not the only vehicle on the road and the person had not got to work before the car was involved in a serious accident in which an out-of-control lorry completely wrote it off, and more or less wrote off the person in it.

The person was taken to hospital and spent several months there whilst the very serious injuries sustained in the accident were attended to. Just before the person was discharged home the doctor came and said: 'We have done what we can, and there is nothing more we can do. You will be completely paralysed for the rest of your life, and never walk, speak or move again. You'll never have children, or sex with your partner, never eat or drink normally, never control your own bowels or bladder or be able to do anything that the able-bodied world considers normal. Just think yourself lucky you are alive.' And with that the doctor left.

The person went home and was nursed there day and night by a kind and caring soul for whom nothing was too much trouble. This nurse did everything, indeed so much so that the person hardly needed even to think about what wanted doing. The nurse concentrated on making the person comfortable and creating a safe, cocooned environment, saying, 'Oh poor, poor you. How I pity you. But worry about nothing, I shall look after you and keep you safe.'

There was a lawyer who visited the person and said: 'You should sue that lorry driver. I could get you millions,' and proceeded to outline the possible court case and its costs and benefits.

There was an MP who visited the person and said: 'This is terrible. Our roads are not safe. I will get a bill through parliament banning lorries like that,' and went on to explain the benefits of the bill.

There was the person's best friend (they had gone to the same school) who visited and said: 'Don't just sit there feeling sorry for yourself. What do these doctors know? Of course you'll walk again, talk again – everything will get back to normal. I heard they know just what to do about problems like this in the USA,' and went on to outline an experimental rehab programme of considerable intensity and dubious methods, and its claimed benefits.

There was a priest who visited the person and said: 'There now, don't be downhearted. After all, God has a plan for us all and I'm sure this would not have happened to you if God didn't mean us to learn something from this experience,' and prayed long and hard about the benefits of suffering.

There was a paraplegic person who had been in the same hospital a few years earlier. They had met in the out-patients' clinic one day. The other paraplegic person said nothing, but aligning the wheels of the two wheel chairs alongside each other, began to go in the same direction as the person who had had the accident.

Which of these – the doctor, the nurse, the lawyer, the MP, the best friend, the priest or the paraplegic person – was a good friend to the person who had had the accident?

If you still have a life, then live.

6. The weary shepherd

As you read this, try to have a 'Wallace and Gromit' style scene in your mind.

There was once a shepherd who was put in charge of a hundred sheep. He was keen and enthusiastic, read the *Shepherd's Manual* regularly and tried to care for his sheep as best he could. Times were hard. Throughout that country sheep were going missing from flocks on a regular basis. No one seemed to know where they went or how or why they got away but almost every flock was diminishing daily.

One evening, as he counted his flock as usual, the shepherd noticed that one sheep was missing. He scanned the whole field and couldn't see it anywhere. He walked all around the sheepfold and it wasn't there. All the other sheep were inside and the shepherd wondered what he should do. Quickly he looked up 'lost sheep' in the *Shepherd's Manual*, but found no help there. Should he go and look for it, or should he stay and look after the other ninety-nine? Eventually, with a heavy heart, he lay down at the door of the sheepfold and stayed to look after the ninety-nine. He slept little, worried as he was about the one lost sheep. Out on the fell the next day he kept looking as he guarded the rest, but he didn't see the lost sheep again.

The rest of the flock were restive and began bleating behind his back. One said: 'That's one gone. I knew this one would be no better at the job than the others.' Another said: 'They're all the same,' and a few began to make life difficult for the shepherd, tripping him up, bumping into him, bleating loudly as he dozed off to sleep and the like.

Others tried to support the shepherd, snuggling up to him at night as he tossed and turned at the door of the sheepfold. The lost sheep did not return.

A week later another sheep went missing. Again he stood at the gate wondering if he should go and look for it, leaving the ninety-eight sheep alone whilst he searched. He thumbed through the *Shepherd's Manual* once more and still got no help there. Weary and confused he lay down and waited for the dawn, alongside the ninety-eight sheep.

The bleating and sabotage by a few of the flock stepped up the following morning, and he got a large bruise when he was tripped up on the way up the fell. He was very tired, not sleeping well for worries about the two lost sheep, and he didn't know what to do.

Over the next few months the situation escalated. The shepherd tried to do his best to look after the flock, keeping to the recommendations of the *Shepherd's Manual*, but more and more sheep went missing in ones and twos, and even threes and fours. The bad-tempered core of the flock got worse and the shepherd received more and more bruises. Every night, after counting in the sheep and finding another had gone, he became increasingly despairing and slept less and less.

Finally the evening came when the numbers in the flock were down to forty-nine – less than half of what he had started with. On that evening he finally decided, after finding no help in the *Shepherd's Manual*, to go and look for the lost sheep. He trugged off up the fell at dusk. He walked all night, further and further from the sheepfold. As the dawn came up he was on a fell he had never visited before. He walked over the crest of the hill and looked into the next valley and got a great surprise. There he saw a valley full of sheep, all happily skipping and playing in a green and beautiful landscape. Amongst the sheep he noted there were wolves and foxes, lions and bears, cows with calves and all sorts of other animals, all playing and living together in the peaceful setting. He scratched his head and wondered if, through lack of sleep, he was seeing things. There was this last chapter in the *Shepherd's Manual* that said shepherds might aspire to such a way of life but he had never seen the likes of it before.

As he stood there wondering what to do next, one of the sheep recognised him and came over. 'Have you come to join us?' he asked enthusiastically. 'You're very welcome to. You'll find all the others here too', he added. Sure enough, as he looked around, the shepherd began to recognise the fifty-one missing sheep of his flock amongst the other animals. He sat down on the grass and tried to think what he should do. He asked the lost sheep to come back with him to the flock. 'No fear!' they bleated together. 'Give all this up for a drafty old sheepfold and that unpleasant flock. You must be joking!' and they all skipped off to play with wolves and whatnot.

He got up wearily and made his way back down the fell and across country to the sheepfold where he had left the sheep. When he got back there was a lot of bad-tempered bleating and some more rough behaviour. He even found sheep poo in his sandwiches. He could have cried, such was the contrast with the beautiful valley he had seen.

Over the next fortnight occasional sheep continued to go missing from the flock but the rate of leaving seemed to have slowed down. In the night he thought he heard some of the bad-tempered sheep threatening the others and trying to frighten them with stories of what really happened to the sheep that went missing. Even so, he was surprised to hear whispers from other sheep about a better place, a peaceful and beautiful place where a sheep could really live. He read the last chapter of the *Shepherd's Manual* many times and struggled to think about what he could do to make it come true in their valley.

During the following months the flock numbers kept falling. Some did go missing, despite the threatening stories of the bad-tempered ones, searching for the new valley they had heard whispered about in the night. Then one night, when the flock was down to twenty sheep, something unexpected happened. One of the sheep who had gone missing a few months previously came back just as the shepherd was getting ready to lie down at the sheepfold door. The sheep nuzzled up to him and whispered, 'Come back to the valley with me,' and set off up the fell. The shepherd looked longingly after the lost sheep that had come back for him but felt torn between his place at the door of the sheepfold and the valley he had seen. He tried to sleep.

The same thing happened the next evening and the next. He even started dreaming about the little sheep and the beautiful valley. It was during the night that he decided to get up and go to find the new valley again. He put his *Shepherd's Manual* and crook by the door of the sheepfold and he stepped out into the night. At first he was hesitant, not sure of the way, but the more he went on the more certain he became, and as the light of dawn began to show in the sky he sensed he was very nearly there. At the top of the hill, with the first rays of the sun breaking over the horizon, he saw the valley spread out before him. The animals were just responding to the first warmth of the sun. As he took it all in, quietly waiting, one of the lost sheep came up to him. 'Welcome back,' it bleated happily. One by one others came and nuzzled him and encouraged him: 'Good to see you.' 'We hoped you'd be back,' and the like. He saw a bear playing with a calf and a lamb trotting along behind a lion. He smiled and stepped into the new valley.

If you have brains, then use them.

7. The badly maintained house [8]

There was once a badly maintained house in a delightful suburb. The people who lived in it were very nice: kind to others, friendly, helpful in the neighbourhood and generous to people in need, even those not in their street. The house itself was in a sorry state. The windows at the front were boarded up, which made the house look dark and uninviting. The front door wasn't at the front, but at the side, and no one coming to the house for the first time would know how to get in; it just wasn't obvious. There was a high narrow gate and an even higher wall that made it almost impossible to see into the garden. The garden itself was over-grown with weeds and the path was a death trap. Besides which the path didn't even lead to the front door but took some round-about overgrown route to the dimly-lit back entrance.

Of course, the people who lived in the house knew all of this. They knew how to avoid the gaps in the path and the brambles. They always took a torch with them and made sure never to try to get in late at night. They often wondered why they didn't have many visitors. They always said they would welcome any who came, but few managed to negotiate the gate, the path and the garden, let alone find the door.

The family got older and older, fewer and fewer. Still they could not understand why more visitors didn't call. What will happen to the house and to the few people who still live in it?

If you have brains, then use them!

8. The woman with the jar of meal

There is a parable in the Gospel of Thomas about a woman with a jar of meal. The following is a paraphrase: [9]

Jesus told this parable: 'The Kingdom of God is like a woman who is carrying a full jar of grain. While she was walking a long way from home, the jar handle broke off and the grain poured out behind her on the road. She did not notice what had happened and carried on walking. When she got home she put the jar down and realised it was empty.'

The parable, and Blessing's discussion of it (see note 9 for reference), appeal to me, linking the story, as she does, to that of the Widow of Zarephath [10] amongst other ideas. Here, in this parable, is a woman doing what millions of women do every day. She is going about the daily business of carrying supplies for her family, heavy but necessary things, in the way of her foremothers: on her head. I remember meeting women on the bridge that crosses the Victoria Falls between Zimbabwe and Zambia. Depending on the way the economy of these two countries is running at the time, the women will be going across the border to buy meal to sell on the other side in order to make a little extra money. They carry the meal in sacks on their heads. Imagine how one of these women would feel if that precious meal had leaked out on the way across the bridge.

This is how I interpret the parable, from my experience.

I am the woman with the jar of meal.
I am carrying the meal for many miles.
It is hot and heavy work.
I am tired out by it,
too exhausted to notice that the meal is leaking out.

The meal is a gift,
a huge and generous gift.
Those waiting for the meal are expecting it.
They think it is for them.
They think it is my job to bring it for them.

The meal represents the gifts of God for the people of God.
It is the church that is waiting for the gift.
It thinks the gift belongs to it by right:
the gifts of God for the people of God.

When I reach the end of the journey with the jar
it is empty.
I am silent.
The church is silent.
No one knows what to say.
Where is the gift?
What has happened to it?

As I look over my shoulder
I see the trail of meal.
It stretches out behind me
into the distance.
All along the route
I see people collecting up the meal;
pouring it into handkerchiefs,
cupping it in their hands.
At first they are glad of the meal.
It is an unexpected treat.
Then they too start to complain:
it is not enough
and they want some more.

Who was the gift of meal really for?
What will happen now the meal has been spilt?
If you have a brain, then use it.

9. The silent woman

Once there was a woman who took shelter in what seemed like a friendly house. She was welcomed in and treated like one of the family and gradually began to see the place as her father's house. One of the sons of the family proposed marriage to her and, confident in her place in the father's house, she accepted. Within a short time of the marriage taking place everything changed. The son was very abusive towards her. He would hit her, beat her and shout at her, in private of course, on a regular basis. She didn't understand his change of mood and personality. She was not able to discuss his behaviour with him; that just made him more violent towards her. She became unsure of her place in the family and did not dare to mention his behaviour to others in the household. She kept silent about the way in which he treated her, covered up the bruises and made excuses so that no one would find out, and thought it must all be her fault, as her husband said.

This went on for several years and the woman became more and more depressed. Eventually the husband announced that he had been asked to take over the role of head of another branch of the family in a city some distance away. So they moved to the new household and the woman hoped this would be a new start for them and their relationship. But it was not. The violence and abuse went on as before, only now the husband was even more careful that no one found out about it, as he was the head of that household. The woman, battered in body, mind and spirit, did not know what to do. She heard of the head of another nearby household and eventually she wrote to him saying something of her circumstances and asking for his help.

When the head of the nearby household got the letter he was shocked. The woman was married to one of his brothers and he couldn't believe what he read. He really didn't know what to do, if anything, about the woman's letter and so he did nothing. Three months went by and he did not reply to the letter the woman had written.

Then a sister from another branch of the family came visiting the brother who had received the letter. Although he had done nothing for three months he was still troubled by what the woman had written. So he showed the letter to his sister and asked her what she thought should be done. Immediately after the sister had read the letter she asked the brother what he had done. 'Nothing' he replied. 'I did not know what to do.'

'Come on and get your coat,' said the sister. 'Where are we going?' asked the brother. 'We are going straight away to see that sister who wrote to you three months ago and see how we can help her.' And so they went.

Of course that is not exactly the end of the story. After a long time, during which other difficulties in finding a new home for the woman had to be overcome and the business of rebuilding her life got under way, the story got in the papers and the husband was thrown out of the household and cast out by the family. But more than that, I wonder what would you do if you got a letter from a member of the household to which you belong that told a story like the one here? Or do you, like so many members of the household, close your mind to the possibility that these things go on in the family. Perhaps you think you will never receive such a letter.

If you have a brain, then use it!

10. Losing it

When I lost it, I didn't know what to do. I was frantic. I had the whole place out several times and still couldn't find it.

Of course, my story often gets left out. Sheep, sons, these are more important in the economy than a widow's pension. But it was important. Vital.

I know our ancestors said the community should help its widows, but these days there seem to be so many of them. How can we help them all? Some remarry, according to the Law, but I'm not sure they are really better off. Most quickly lose everything. Family members take their possessions, claiming the widows have no rights to things that belong to the family. Sometimes they promise to help and then neglect to do anything.

A widow needs her own security.

I had mine: ten coins should last a while at least.

Then I lost one.

I'd lost things in the house before. Over the years there had been one or two searches for odd household items I'd mislaid. I knew the places where they usually turned up.

This time was different. It just wasn't to be found anywhere. After looking all day I said to myself, 'It will turn up,' and tried to sleep. But I couldn't. I kept thinking of places to look, and in the end there was nothing for it but to get up and look there. By the morning I had slept little and felt dreadful. My anxiety had grown in the night and was now a looming shadow in the corner of each room.

All the next day, I kept looking. It must be here somewhere. What a lot of stuff I had, most of it unnecessary. I moved piles of things around and sorted through them time after time. I forgot to eat. I was obsessed with finding it.

After several days of this it was clear that rather than finding the coin, I was actually losing my mind. I couldn't sleep. I didn't eat or wash. I just kept looking.

Eventually one of my neighbours noticed something was not quite right and asked me what was wrong. I mumbled incoherently and continued my searching. She said she'd come and help me. I didn't really notice at first, but after a while she went for her sister, and she also came to help. Then her sister-in-law brought her mother and pretty soon all the women in the street had come to help, each with a broom.

That's when we began to organise ourselves. We swept out each room from top to bottom. I was calmer now. The presence of my neighbours dispelled the monster shadows in the heaps of things and in the corners. Their cheerful voices made the rooms hum and sing, which is something that had not happened for some time.

As we swept each room we told each other stories of things we'd lost. One would say, 'I remember losing it,' and go on to tell a tale about something precious. Not everyone's tale had what you might call a happy ending. Sometimes we just stood silently, leaning on our brooms, catching our breath and acknowledging the pain and sorrow of one who had lost a baby in early pregnancy, or a child, or … It was at times like that when my thoughts for my lost coin, my security as I saw it, changed. Perhaps I could live without it after all.

It was late in the afternoon when we got onto the last room. Each woman was thinking about the meal she needed to cook back in her own house. No one wanted to be the first to say they could spare no more time to help. We did the last room as thoroughly as the rest.

And there it was. Even now no one seems to remember who found it. As we swept and swept great clouds of dust and demons, a metallic sound drew all our eyes and there it was spinning gaily in the centre of the room. We watched it with our mouths open. It stopped spinning and sat there winking at us in the last rays of the day.

What a cheer went up. Each woman shouted for joy and hugged her neighbour. Very soon we were dancing, like at a wedding, round and round and round that room, at last sinking down on the floor and laughing.

I got some grapes and some nuts. We quickly made some flat bread. There was a bit of cheese, some figs and a jar of water. It was a feast. I hadn't eaten such good things in such wonderful company for ages. We talked and passed the coin around. Each woman lifted it high and kissed it, saying a blessing for me: 'To the future.'

I'd lost it. It had been a frightening time. I'd lost more than the coin before I had, unexpectedly, found much more. No – not the junk in my house, but the love and friendship in my street and the blessing of all those women.

If you have a brain, then use it.

11. Poppies

*Imagine a field of green wheat and red poppies
on a summer's day, or spend some time looking
at a reproduction of Monet's painting 'Les
coquelicots à Argenteuil'.*

The poppies really make the field.
Without the poppies the field would be green;
just green.
Stunning enough in a season when green
seems more vibrant than ever.
But the poppies really make the field.
See how they line its edges
and wander into the centre,
shooting up scarlet surprises
at unlikely intervals.
Yes, the poppies really make the field,
but too many parables of 'wheat and tares'
stop us taking them in.
Look again.
Absorb it all, green and scarlet.
The poppies *are* the field.
When harvest time comes,
it takes all stalks. [11]

12. Still growing

In these words
and silences,
we make stories.
Some of them are true.
Some of them really happened.
Some of them are what we wish for,
wait for, yearn for, hope for.
God the story-teller,
help us to sort out the threads.
God the story-keeper,
add them to your store.
God the story-maker,
keep us alive to your words in us.
Take the smallest seed of faith,
that together we may nurture it,
and know it is still growing.

NOTES

1   W. R. Herzog (1994).

2   See pages 46-47 and 97-98 for material about the story of Ruth.

3   Rebecca Squires is a member of Shiregreen United Reformed Church (quotation used with permission).

4   Reece Philips is a member of Shiregreen United Reformed Church (quotation used with permission).

5   First appeared in *Harvest for the World* compiled by Geoffrey Duncan (Christian Aid/Canterbury Press, 2002, pages 86-88).

6   For Gwen.

7   For 'Together for Regeneration', Sheffield.

8   From *Shining Faces*, the prayer handbook for 2000-2001, published by the United Reformed Church, 2000, used by permission.

9   Based on a translation in Kamila Blessing (2002) 'The Woman Carrying the Jar of Meal', in Mary Ann Beavis (ed) (2002), *The Lost Coin: Parables of Women, Work and Wisdom*, pages 158-173.

10   I Kings 17:8-16.

11   Inspired by a field of poppies and the Burngreave Monday Club, a day centre for people with learning difficulties.

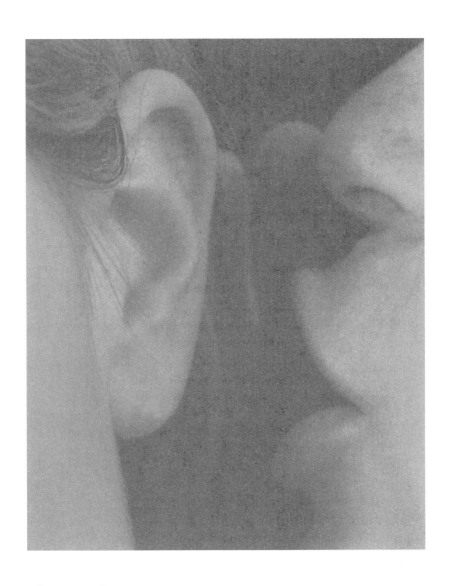

Chapter four

From the edge of the Bible

It is in combining the strategies we have shared in new and creative ways that we find the new voices to tell new stories that take us on new journeys. Amongst those who speak to us in new voices, who tell new stories and invite us to accompany them on new journeys are people who are on the edge of the Bible: the marginal voices in the written text and its traditional interpretations. A more winsome way of using the Bible is to make the characters come alive so that they relate to the ordinary world of ordinary people. This involves identifying those people in the texts who are like those whom you live alongside. Some of these may be named in the written text and many more will be anonymous, both women and men. Even more will be the silent, anonymous people at the edges of the text.

Begin by making a list of people that the group identify as winsome, or attractive, in some way. Encourage people to say what it is that attracts them to these characters and to voice what the silences are behind the Bible stories in which they feature. A possible list from the gospels might include: [1]

the boy with the lunch
the bread-maker
the coin-loser
Peter's mother-in-law
Andrew's mother-in-law
Jairus's daughter
Joanna
the lepers who didn't come back
the woman who anointed Jesus
the women who followed Jesus
the women who stood at the cross
Zachariah
Zebedee

With the possible exception of Andrew's mother-in-law, each can be matched to the written text in at least one of the gospels. Many more could also be identified.

As far as the parables of Jesus are concerned, it is reasonable to postulate that to some extent he based the characters in them on real people. How else would these stories have resonated so well with locals that they were memorable enough to be handed on? The characters can be brought alive through story-telling. Sometimes the same person or character tells more than one story, hence the two stories of the woman with the yeast in this section. The idea is not to tell the story word for word or read it out in a wooden way. Rather it is important to get into the story and tell it your own way. What is written here is intended only as a starting point and a possible guide.

1. Naomi, Orpah, Boaz and Ruth

I am Naomi.
I was bitter.
A woman has little enough security here,
even when married,
but a widow is worth nothing.
I had to go home.
I couldn't expect them to come with me.
There would be no more sons from my womb.
As I see it, Ruth went further than any mother-in-law
could have expected.

I am Orpah.
I was silent.
I knew that I did not have to go with Naomi,
but I wasn't sure about going home either.
We had survived so much and
they were almost all the support I had left.
No one could say which way offered the most security.
As I see it, Ruth made her choice and I made mine.

I am Boaz.
I was moved.
I'd heard about Naomi's plight
and about her loyal daughter-in-law.
I was surprised when I first saw her in my field
and more surprised still when she turned up one night.
I wasn't used to such forward behaviour
but it made a pleasant change to meet someone
with her own opinions.
I quickly began to respect her.

As I see it, Ruth was the partner I had been waiting for.

I am Ruth
I was ready.
I know I didn't have to go with Naomi.
I know I took lots of other risks,
going to the fields, following Naomi's advice.
I was surprised when Boaz noticed me,
and more surprised still about what followed.
I feared I had gone too far and would be sold like a field
but Boaz kept his word.
As I see it, for me, Ruth, my journey goes on in faith and in love.

All:
This is the story we shared.
This is how we tell it.
What is your story?
How will you tell it?

How to use Naomi, Orpah, Ruth and Boaz

1. Dress up (not the nativity play curtains), interpreting the characters according to those you meet in your community.

2. Use the words as a conclusion to a remembering or reading of the story of the book of Ruth.

3. Use the story to introduce a reflection on a new sense of direction, or evaluation of a project or activity.

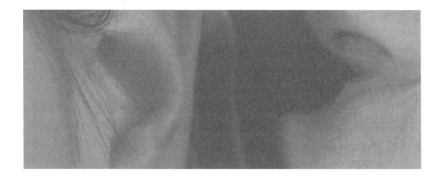

2. Chloe [2]

I'm Chloe from Corinth. It's a busy seaport and as a result Corinth is a thriving commercial centre. I'm a widow. My husband had a well run shipping business and so I'm quite a rich widow – a sort of first-century Jackie Onassis! And my life could have remained rich and comfortable. After all, I have a nice villa and plenty of slaves and enough money to last a lifetime.

But I was never satisfied with that, even before my husband's death – well, all my adult life really. I know I've been searching for something. At first I thought it was enough to find some sort of personal harmony; a sort of inner peace. I tried all sorts of different cults: Apollo, Isis and other local favourites. Then I was attracted to Judaism. I got a Greek version of their scriptures and went to hear some of their teachers discuss them. That was fascinating. I realised that I was looking for more than just a personal harmony. I wanted a better community and a better way of life for us all, me and my whole household.

A Jewish teacher came to Corinth with a new message. Jesus, a Jew, had been crucified by the Roman authorities in Jerusalem, but he'd risen from the dead three days later. It was compelling stuff as he talked about what this Jesus had said and done and about his followers.

There was a small group of these Christians, as they called themselves, forming in Corinth. Women were equally welcome and I joined them. Later Paul came and told us the whole story. I and my household are now a branch of this group, a house church you might say. There are several all over the city. Of course, we're quite a diverse group. People come from all different backgrounds. There's bound to be different opinions, arguments, disputes. Most of the time these are fairly harmless but occasionally some get more serious!

You see, our different backgrounds mean we understand the gospel differently. Some say it's all right to carry on your life as before, after you become a Christian. Now, many of our members are rich and just as many are their slaves. In some households relationships have not changed. The masters still treat the slaves badly, claiming it's a God-given relationship. Some of us have challenged this. In my household we try to aim for all to be equal. We run things together and the old divisions are no longer relevant. You'd probably call it a commune. Of course, others say it won't work or it won't last but we're committed to being a community of equals. Others want to reinforce the old hierarchies so much that they make silly claims. One group claimed they were better Christians than another group, because Apollos baptised them, and another group said they were because Paul did it! My household appealed to Paul to put an end to this, although he wasn't here at the time and he couldn't remember whom he had baptised anyway! As he rightly said, it is irrelevant. What matters is that we are all Christ's people, a community committed to living in his way, like a body with many parts, although I expect we shall go on arguing about what exactly that means!

We get people coming along just to the celebration of the 'Lord's Supper'; they think it's a free party. Not all our members agree with this, preferring a more solemn occasion. But if people are hungry, they're bound to look for food.

Another group wanted women to cover their heads in worship. They thought we'd get a bad name if people confused us with some other local cults. This problem was more difficult to deal with; some of us were not so ready to compromise. We appealed to Paul again, and even he couldn't seem to make up his mind, giving some rather conflicting advice. Mind you, I notice it's not something you worry about here now. I told Paul it would never catch on.

As leaders we meet together from time to time, trying to discern the right thing to do here. Some of our groups go their own way on an issue, others close when energy ebbs away and the group dies, whilst others are growing. I hold on to what Paul taught us: that we should be united in mind and of the same purpose. It's not easy to achieve, as I've tried to show you, but it's a struggle worth being committed to. It's one I hope we witnesses at Corinth will be remembered for.

How to use Chloe's story

This story can be used in a number of ways as a background or introduction to:

1. a series on the letters to the church at Corinth;

2. gender issues in the early church and the church today;

3. as an introduction to vision building or development in the local church.

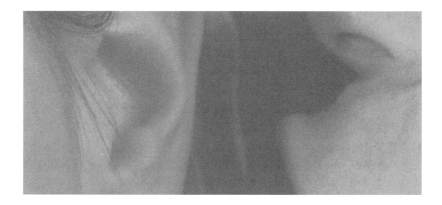

3. The four Marys

One evening between Easter and Pentecost, in an upper room....

There were four of us in the room that evening, and we were waiting. We'd all done our fair share of that one way and another. There was Mary his mother, whose body must have ached for all the waiting she'd done with him from conception, through birth, life and death. What was compelling about her was how she made us all feel as if waiting with her was what we most wanted to do right then.

Mary had come from Bethany, without Martha this time – although Martha's obvious absence meant we couldn't help but think of her with us, in a way. As usual, Mary was silent, with her most expressive face and body the clue to all that was, for her, unspeakable.

Mary who was married to Cleopas had not returned to Emmaus with him this time; after they had told their story she'd decided to stay in Jerusalem and wait with us. And I had also decided to stay. In all the confused coming and going of the last few weeks, this seemed to be the place to be. Peter and James had invited me back to Galilee but, even though the green hills and the lakes were an inviting prospect, I couldn't quite bring myself to go.

Although we had not said so openly, we seem to have agreed between us that we would wait here. As we did so, occasionally a story or song would fill the silence. We'd go about our daily business, keep each other company, and reflect on all that had happened while we'd travelled with him.

There was a lot to think about and a pressing need to try to make sense of it all. Mary his mother spoke about the many times she had found herself crossing the lines of social convention because of him: from the very first decision to go ahead with the pregnancy, to the very last to stand on the exposed hill and wait for the end.

Mary of Emmaus too had found conventions challenged as she and Cleopas had decided together to go with him, to welcome him and some of us into their homes and how they had shared in the welcoming, the serving and the listening. I could see that Mary of Bethany was agreeing with her, though she'd not break her silence to say so. She leant forward, towards the other Mary, encouraging her to say more, for the story held echoes of her own and by her posture she confirmed this. The home at Bethany had also been a place of welcome in which roles were shared and people were valued, although Martha, had she been there, would probably have been the first to say how he had made a particular contribution to its development, affirming each one of them as he had: the verbal and the non-verbal ones.

I could remember moments from our journeys – short bits of conversations, long silences. I tried to piece all this together and include something of what those other absent friends might have added had they been there. I knew we all had many different thoughts and views about him and it was good to have a chance to reflect on their diversity. A phrase kept echoing in my head: 'He has overcome the world.' It sounded like the kind of thing Peter or James or John might have said. It niggled at me because I know I was struggling to see it their way. Even my experiences since his death didn't make it all that much clearer to me. I was, like all of us, missing him now.

To overcome the world would take more than this: death at the hands of corrupt political forces and an early morning encounter I could hardly put into words. I listened further to the others. Mary from Emmaus was saying again how she'd know it was him when he broke the bread – he'd done it so often, you see. Her story was both compelling and comforting. Once again Mary of Bethany encouraged her from within her silent response and his mother agreed. 'I can almost smell the bread as you tell us about it,' she said.

I smiled and went to the window. In a way I was also beginning to miss the rest of them too. Would they come back from Galilee and if so when? How long would we wait and for what? Signs were the weather was changing; clouds were building up and it was likely the wind would swing around soon. What might a change in the weather bring? I shivered and thought I was glad to be in Jerusalem rather than in a boat on an unpredictable lake if we were in for a gale.

I let my mind fast forward a bit, recognising that there would be a time when this would be the past and we would be telling old stories about it all. There would be a time when we'd have moved on and things would have fallen into place. I wouldn't always miss him quite like this. We'd find a way forward: new roles, new opportunities. Perhaps even cryptic sayings would make sense eventually.

I turned round to face the others: compelling Mary, the mother; silent Mary of Bethany; exuberant Mary of Emmaus and me, Mary of Magdala, the story-teller. Four Marys who had travelled with him to … to where? To here. We looked at each other and there and then we promised to journey on together, after the wind changed.

How to use the story of the four Marys

1. As part of a series of studies on the women of the New Testament.

2. At a quiet, reflective service of worship sometime between Easter and Pentecost.

3. As a reflection for people living with bereavement and loss.

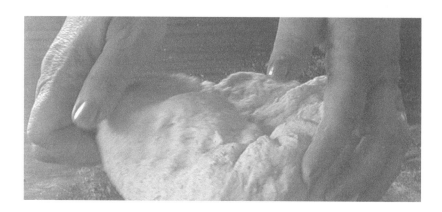

4. The leper's companion

During the story the woman takes a bowl of flour and yeast, mixes it with water and kneads it together 3 while she is talking.

Of course I knew he was different when he came back. It was obvious to anyone who'd known him as long and as intimately as I had. I knew every scab, every scar on his body. To find his skin was different, like a newborn baby, was amazing. I couldn't say anything at first.

It was he himself who broke the silence. 'We saw the healer,' he said. 'All ten of us.' They had set out that morning to find this healer, Jesus of Nazareth, who was so talked about. They were ten from this leper colony – some newcomers, some old hands – who decided to go and see for themselves. It was Nathan who had talked them into it. He was a newcomer and had not quite settled down; still angry, wanting to be back in his own village; he'd try anything, he said. Not all of the others were so convinced. Like my Amos, many had made new relationships, a new start even out here in the middle of nowhere.

Amos and I had been together quite a few years now. He'd been alone when I met him. I'd stumbled across the lepers on my own rush to obscurity. I was running away from a stoning mob at the time and they certainly weren't in the mood for listening to my side of the story. Amos listened and over time our friendship developed and our new family began. I didn't have leprosy then, of course. I do now.

So when he said he'd go with them I was surprised, as we'd both agreed long since to stay together here and make the most of it. He said he was only going to keep an eye on them and to see what this Jesus was like.

He told me what had happened. They had come across Jesus and his group and, getting as close as they dared, had listened to what he said. Amos had wanted to listen more; Jesus spoke in a new way, with authority, he said, about love for our neighbours, however different they were from us. But some of the others had wanted to get on with it. Nathan especially was impatient. He urged them forward and once the crowd spotted them, they made way for the whole group, falling back with the usual blend of fear and revulsion even our former friends and families commonly display.

It seems they didn't know what to say when Jesus asked them what they wanted and it was Amos who found himself speaking for them all. 'We've heard about you, we've listened to what you said. Our neighbours have rejected us. There's no way back for us, unless …' As his words had trailed off, Nathan had interrupted: 'We want to be healed,' he had shouted.

Jesus had looked at each one of them. He had seen the scars and the memories etched into the skin of each member of the group. 'You are clean,' he said to them. 'Go and do what the Law demands.' They were surprised it was so simple. They got up and started to walk away, looking at each other in bewilderment. Halfway up the road, Nathan let out a shriek: 'He's done it, he's really done it!' And then he started running back, back towards Jesus. They heard him saying: 'Wait, wait, I'm coming with you.'

As the other nine made their way back to us, some started to wonder out loud what might happen now; others kept their thoughts to themselves. Ruben was the first to arrive. He gathered up his things and hurried away from Naomi, leaving her sobbing in the dust as he disappeared into the distance, back to the village he had come from so many years ago.

Over the next few days a few of the others left. Some of the families moved to other parts of the camp. But at least half the group did not leave. They met each morning as they used to, and sometimes they talked and sometimes they just sat. They were perplexed. What should they do now?

Amos and I talked about it all long into the night. In the end he decided to go back and find Jesus and listen to some more of what he had to say. He did this on and off for a few months, going for a week or so and then returning to tell us what had happened and what Jesus had said. The stories he told went around the camp and more and more came to listen to his reports. Others went to see Jesus and some of them got healed too. Some of those who did asked Amos why he kept coming back to the camp. After all, he didn't have leprosy now. Why didn't he just go back to the village he had come from before. 'Before what?' he would say. They would lower their eyes and there would be an uncomfortable moment.

We'd agreed we would stay. I still had leprosy so we couldn't return together, and I didn't want to return anyway. What if the mob still remembered? We agreed we would stay and we would tell the stories Amos had heard Jesus tell and we would try to work out what they meant and how our camp could be a neighbourly and welcoming place, against all the odds. And we did.

There it is [*holds up the dough*], all leavened.

How to use the story of the leper's companion

1. With the remembered Bible study of the nine unhealed lepers (pages 34-37).

2. In a series introducing the parables or characters from the parables.

3. In a series exploring anonymous people from the gospels.

4. In a discussion about inclusion, and who or what defines who is included or excluded.

5. Preparing the feast: Woman with the leaven [4]

This story can be used to help 'remember the narrative' of the Lord's Supper if you follow the directions in italics as you tell the story.

As you are speaking, take a bowl containing flour, yeast, salt, oil and warm water and mix them together to make a dough.

People ask me when this all began, and you'll all have your own answers to that, I know. Some will say it began the day he rose, that very same evening when we all got together again and each of us told our stories. That was the first time we celebrated it like he said we should, remembering him. Some will say it began those few evenings before, that dreadful night he was arrested. We'd been unsuspecting – well, some of us. Perhaps it is nearer the truth to say we all suspected and mostly each other. The days and weeks and months had taken their toll on our ragged community. We were depleted in numbers and in energy. We argued about everything, even where to hold the Passover. He sorted it out – told us where to find the place and the sign, a man with a water jar on his head – well, that one certainly had us laughing.

The evening itself was a mix of subdued anticipation, exhaustion and questioning. He washed our feet, something I'd done many times – but him doing it? Peter wasn't the only one who had questions about that but most of us kept them to ourselves, as ever. Judas got up and left, but then people were always coming and going. We thought no more of it, until much later.

Pause here to wipe your hands on damp cloth, setting bowl aside for later.

Take some already baked bread and the wine already poured from the table.

Like I said, most people think it began there – bread and wine on the Passover table, plagues numbered, Elijah saluted again. The bread in his hands, just like I've held it in mine so often, soft on the inside, hard on the outside. The wine, rich and deep and red, running like blood. He took them and cradled them and shared them: his body to be broken, his blood to be poured out. Something he wanted us all to remember.

Sweeping up the crumbs much later, I remembered it and that's why I say it didn't begin there. It could have been in Martha's house – she always laid on plenty of food – or that time at Peter's house when his mother-in-law had been ill but still insisted on getting the meal ready. It could have been in his own home, alongside Mary and Joseph and his brothers and sisters every day of his life for the thirty-odd years before he took to the road. It could have been on the road itself, around campfires lit in dark places, or in the frugal meals shared with poor households all over Galilee and Judea. After all, it is such an everyday thing, isn't it: to share bread and remember?

Refer back to the bowl of dough again: knead it a little more.

But I like to think it goes right back, through the generations of our ancestors, past that desert journey and Passover flight – after all we'd no leaven then. Right back to the beginning, when a woman first took yeast and mixed it with flour and set it to rise. It was a deep knowledge, like the knowledge that created the world and all that is in it, shared with our ancestors for good or evil. Sometimes we choose right. Sometimes we choose good and the yeast rises and the dough feeds us again.

Take up the baked bread again and break it as the words are said:

And for that I thank God: for the flour, for the yeast, for the dough, for the baking and the breaking, for the remembering.

How to use this story

This story is written so that it can be used at the place of the narrative of the Lord's Supper and the Prayer of Thanksgiving in an informal communion service.

6. Downhill to Jerusalem

Our son had been going downhill for some time. Since his early childhood, as other children were learning, he seemed always to be finding things more difficult. He would have these moments when he seemed not to be himself: his eyes would roll and his limbs would shake. Sometimes this happened for just a few moments, sometimes much longer, but every time it seemed to me like a lifetime. Afterwards he would be sleepy and slow; he would stumble and dribble and gradually come back to himself. But over the years these moments took control of his life – they were longer and more frequent, and the effects lasted and meant he learnt less and less. What he had learnt he forgot or seemed unable to do any more. We were losing him and we didn't know how to stop it happening.

My husband tried to ignore it at first. He told me I was making a fuss and that there was nothing wrong. He wasn't there to hold him during the shaking attacks or clean him up after he messed himself. My friends and family were embarrassed for me. They wouldn't speak about it and turned away if they happened to be nearby when it happened.

Strangers would express their opinions. 'What sinners you and your husband must be,' one told me once. Many told me, 'It is the will of God,' and how I hated their God who had this awful will to blight this little life and mine too.

I had cried so much over the years that there was nothing left in me: no tears, no love, no life. I had dried up and just went on waking and sleeping through habit, nothing more. The boy too seemed empty. There was nothing left of him either. There was nothing he could do for himself; I did it all for him. And yet still he lived, if you could call it life.

Someone in my husband's family told him about a teacher and healer from Nazareth and convinced him to try to see him. I was surprised. In all this time my husband had shown little or no interest in the boy, let alone any concern about whether or not he could be helped. But people said this healer had done wonderful things and there were many stories about him going around the neighbourhood. So we went to the place where he was said to be.

My husband arranged everything. I just went along, in the cart, holding my son in my lap, but when we got there the healer was not there.

It seems he had gone up a mountain with some of his followers. He used to do that when he wanted to pray, others said. No one had any idea how long he would be gone, but we were not alone in waiting for him at the bottom of the mountain. The weather was strange for the time of year: very muggy and heavy and there was a lot of thunder, but no rain, as if something was about to break but no one knew what it might be.

There were some there who tried to help us as we waited. Some women tried to make us comfortable. One held my son for me as I got down from the cart; held him like I would. Another got us some water so I could wash him and also shared some bread with us. A few came to listen to our story. My husband told them we wanted to see the healer because our son had this strange illness that came on him and made him shake for no reason. They said little but clearly didn't know what to do. I said nothing.

Eventually we had word that the healer was coming: coming down from the mountain with his friends. A buzz went around the group and the buzz grew into a roar. As he got nearer some went up to him, tried to touch him, screamed for his help. My husband and I watched amazed. We didn't move. The women who had helped us, and the men who had listened, brought the healer over to us. 'This is the family who wants to see you,' they said. 'We didn't know what to do.'

His face was bright and warm. I looked at him and for the first time in all of this I dared to let my heart hope a little. He sat with us and listened to my husband. By now he was very distressed. I had never seen him like that but it was as if all the waiting had finally brought to the surface everything he had never allowed himself to think or feel or say in all those years. He was crying as he told the story of how our son had changed from being like any other child to this helpless and almost lifeless individual who could only shake and dribble and shit.

The healer held my husband's arm as his crying made his own speech more and more incoherent. 'Only believe,' was all the healer said. What did it mean? My husband looked at the hand on his arm and then at the healer's face. 'Oh, I believe,' he said, and surely he was as faithful a person as anyone you might meet. 'I do believe,' he repeated, 'but help my unbelief.' These last words were just a groan.

Then the healer looked at me. He didn't ask me anything and no words passed between us. He just looked at me as I held the boy in my lap and as he looked it was as if he knew the whole story, as if he understood how the tears had dried up, and why, and how my life had been turned into an empty husk. 'This is his mother,' one of the women said. His face acknowledged what she had said but no one else said anything for a very long time.

Eventually I understood that he wanted to hold the boy himself. He sat as I had been sitting on the ground and took him on his own lap. Very few people ever held him. He would go very stiff if you held him wrong or if he didn't take to you, so mostly it was just me that held him. I wondered what would happen as I put my son in his arms, but the boy did not stir. He sat with him in his lap, just like I did myself most days, just sat there for quite some time. Gradually my husband stopped crying and looked up.

As we all sat there together, I felt myself relax. People started to move away and some from his group began to get a meal together. We remained where we were, the three adults and the boy on the healer's lap as life went on around us. After a while my husband took his sleeve and wiped our son's face, moving the hair off of his forehead gently with his fingers. He had not done that in a long time. I moved closer to my husband and we both looked at our son lying there relaxed and seemingly content – at least not agitated like he was quite often.

The sun began to go down and the food was ready. The members of his group brought it over to where we were sitting and began to pass it around. The healer took a few pieces and we were also given some. It was simple stuff: bread, figs, cheese and the like. There was some talking in low voices as the evening drew on. A fire had been kindled in the middle of the group, and we just sat there dozing and listening. People began to wrap themselves up in their cloaks around the fire, obviously intending to sleep just where they were. The healer wrapped his cloak around our son, and laid him between us as we too, wrapped up in our own thoughts, rested by the fire. We listened to the sounds of the night, but it all seemed very peaceful and we slept.

The next morning the group got up, ready to go on. They were going to Jerusalem we heard, but we knew we couldn't go with them. We climbed back onto the cart. The healer put my son back into my arms and waved to us as we started back to our village. Eventually he turned around and began walking downhill to Jerusalem.

So, you'll be wondering how that changed anything, anything at all. As if it could. As if a trip to see a magic man could make a difference to such a hopeless situation. But it did. My husband was changed by it. He would talk now, about his son, about the time we saw the healer, and he would help me. He would even hold the boy, like I did, like the healer had done, and help me with the things that our son needed. Our son was changed, though not cured exactly. He would still shake and moan at times, but generally he seemed calmer. I had changed. I remembered the eyes of the healer as they looked into mine. I remembered him holding my boy just like I did. I remembered him listening, just listening. It had changed us all. We could work together. We could be together.

As for the healer, I didn't hear about him for some time. It was long after Passover when a story started going around that something terrible had happened in Jerusalem that year. The healer had been arrested, tortured and crucified. Someone said they'd even seen his mother holding her son's lifeless body.

I knew just how she felt.

Opportunities to use this story

1. With the Bible study of the Transfiguration and the boy with epilepsy on page 40.

2. When exploring the experiences of families of disabled children.

3. During a week to raise awareness of people with epilepsy.

4. When exploring the stories of silent and unnamed women in the Bible.

7. Called as women

Holy One, you call us,
and we wonder whether we are coming or going.
As Naomi, Ruth and Orpah journeyed together,
so we too struggle with our sense of direction.
As the women waited at the cross,
so we too look into the future in worry and wonder.
As Phoebe, Prisca and Lydia all contributed their gifts
to the early church
so we too bring our contribution in love and worship.

Forgive our backward glances,
our constant looking over our shoulders,
our harping on about yesterday's ways.

Fill us with a sense of your presence in the present,
for we too are alive now
and we celebrate new life and new opportunities.

NOTES

[1] This list was generated by a group at the Urban Theology Unit in December 1998.

[2] You may want to dress up in something long and flowing to play Chloe and cover your hair (not the nativity play curtains again – please), or dress like Jackie Onassis.

[3] The actual ingredients you use will depend on whether you intend to make this into something edible afterwards.

[4] For Meersbrook Park United Reformed Church, Easter 2005.

Part three

Words for worship

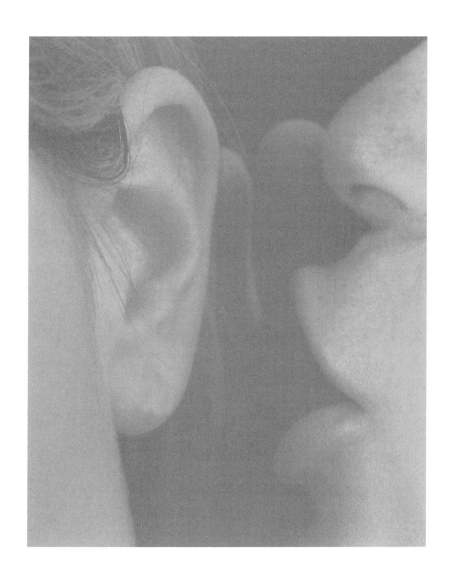

Chapter five

Mondays God

Mondays God

The God I meet on Monday
is putting up 'open' signs in the high street.
The God I meet on Tuesday
translates my hesitant words into another language.
The God I meet on Wednesday
feeds hungry ones at the lunch club.
The God I meet on Thursday
is growing people at the toddler group.
The God I meet on Friday
is building a new highway through the wasteland.
The God I meet on Saturday
is breaking new ground on the allotment.
The God I meet on Sunday
is not different.

Quick fit

It's the tracking again –
way out this time.
The dials swing round
and the instruments
tell their story.
Oil and grease,
bumps and jerks,
all play their part.
Jacked up for all to see –
I confess
it's ages since I had it done.
On a bench in the corner
I try to keep out of the way
as the sweeper comes round.

With dirty hands
and stained overalls
the ministry of
getting me back on track
is under way.
Adjustments are made,
safety is checked.
I am touched by these shared concerns.
'That's it, luv,
all done now.'
Go in peace.

Human communication [1]

The universe pulses with the potential for communication;
from star to star, from cell to cell,
communication is both mystery and reality.
Recognising this diversity in a myriad species,
we concern ourselves with human communication
the mind-expanding diversity of which is huge enough.

We work together to enable
the everyday business of getting by
at the bus stop or in the post office queue,
at the board meeting or in the classroom.

We acknowledge that playing with words
and weaving with silence is not a level playing field.
Social circumstances are such that these
may marginalise rather than empower
both individuals and groups.
We are committed to the struggle
for a just fulfilment of each person's potential.

Urban Psalm 23

God is my lollipop lady: [2]
I am safe with her.
She sees me across the busy junction
to find a safe place to relax.
She restores my faith in humanity
as she helps me to choose
the right time and place to cross.
Even though this road is notorious
she is here, night and morning,
and I'm not afraid to cross with her.
Even the snarling engines draw back
as she prepares a safe passage.
I cross readily and we exchange greetings.
The encouragement and love that surround me
help me to grow in self-worth and confidence
and I shall take the risk of making
many more crossings in her company.

The narrow gate [3]

Go in by the narrow gate.

It's the same for us all,
bloody and bawling,
sliding uncontrollably into reality,
powerless and vulnerable:
we all came in by the narrow gate.

Go on by the narrow gate.

It's a choice for us all,
bloody but not bowed,
alternately plunging and climbing,
powerless and vulnerable:
we can all choose whether to go on by the narrow gate.

Christ of the narrow gate,
how many times have you been there before me?

Creator of the birthing moment,
how many times have you been there before me?

Spirit of risk-taking,
how many times have we been here now?

Silent or speaking,
alive not dead,
I choose once again to
go on in by the narrow gate.

Dealing in death

God of life,
forgive us for dealing in death
as we turn our back on our neighbours
and once again sink into the apathy
of dried-up religion.
As we take our next breath
may it be a holy inspiration
which fires us up to come out of our tombs
and live the life of your kin and kingdom.

Rising [4]

Seagulls rise
over landfill sites
and beaches,
wherever we dump our rubbish;
waste of wealth
and flotsam of riches.

Planets rise
over countless skies
beyond the stars;
burnt out gas giants
run rings around suns,
meteorites mark moons.

Chests rise
labouring for each breath;
flailing arms fail to grasp opportunities;
cells divide
and carry our rubbish
to another generation.

Body-wise God
may we rise,
>with seagulls through the clouds;
>with planets beyond horizons;
>with chests filled by each breath.

Shaky buildings [5]

God of cell, spore and microbe,
now the dry rot is here,
help us to see this invasion
as a positive contribution to our plans.
In the meetings, the form-filling
and the building work that lie ahead
may we grasp new opportunities.
May the life-giving we share here
be as infectious as this fungus.

NOTES

1 Written for the Department of Human Communication Sciences, University of Sheffield, in memory of Jo Hubbard, who was a student there.

2 Outside schools in the UK, morning and evening, there is usually a school crossing patrol, affectionately called 'the lollipop lady' for the large 'lollipop' she carries which says 'Stop, Children Crossing'. This psalm relates to Hatfield Primary School, Sheffield.

3 Thanks to Ruth Weston for her inspiring narrative on subversive child-birth at the Urban Theology Unit in July 2003.

4 Written for Women in Ministries, January 2004.

5 After finding the dry rot at St James URC: thanks to my father for all his help.

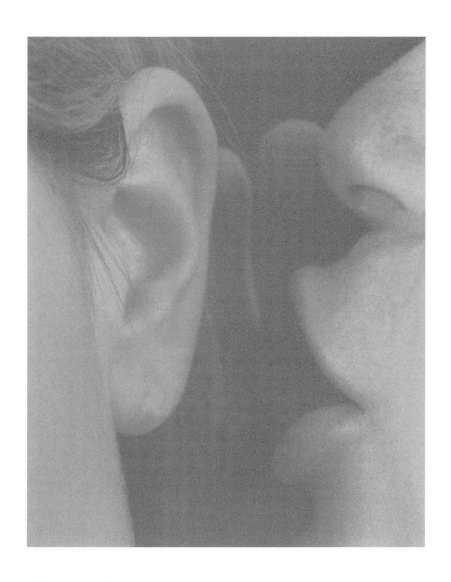

Chapter six

Show me the life

Common enough

Did Jesus
catch 'flu
from Peter's
mother-in-law?

Was his childhood
a long succession
of ear infections
accompanied by
hearing loss?
If you have ears,
what then?

Did eye infections
bring blindness into focus,
or itchy skin
make the link to leprosy?

When head throbs
and joints ache,
do we really think
that his was a life
without the common cold,
the threat of virus or bacteria?

Only One
who had
a real body
could touch
another.

Only One
who knew
its frailty
could say
'This is my body'
and mean it.

A place for anger

Author of anger, I'm screaming again!
Around me injustice and people in pain,
a world so unequal I cry out in rage:
so tired and frustrated, I'm locked in a cage.

Christ of the temple, where tables were turned,
to end exploitation you also have yearned.
I open my anger and show it to you:
the hurt and the weeping are hiding there too.

Spirit of Wisdom, you shout in the street,
a challenge to people wherever they meet.
Not quiet acquiescence but passionate voice,
your presence affirms that I've made a sound choice.

God of emotions, the ups and the downs,
of shouting and whispers, of smiling and frowns,
I'm hoping for wholeness in your fierce embrace,
there's room in your love to give anger a place.

Tune: Slane (10.11.11.12)

Not here

His body is not here.

There is a body here,
but it's not his.
At least, I don't think it is.
It claims his name
and has some residual features
that suggest a family likeness
but it's not his.

Besides which, this body
is barely alive.

It hardly breathes,
it scarcely moves,
it struggles to remain conscious
to all of the world around.

So where is he?
Lost, decades back,
centuries even,
by continual cell division?
Or did he, like so many,
just get up and leave,
when it all got so deathly?

As I stand gawping
at the gaping tomb,
I wonder where to look first.

On the streets

Jesus Christ is waiting, waiting in the streets ... [1]

Waiting One,
where stones are thrown
and bad words hurled;
where petrol bombs ignite
and plastic bullets ricochet;
be there, between the factions,
not on one side or the other,
but with your generous arms flung wide
and your scarred hands exposed,
showing us what it costs
to answer the question
'Who is my neighbour?'

Bodies of risk

For each reflection of ourselves
    that we reject in each other:
        our longing for intimacy
        inhibited by our confining of sexuality,
        our longing for wholeness
        inhibited by our confining of disability,
        our longing for the full stature of Christ,
        inhibited by our confining religiosity;
    only your love can liberate us.
Plunge us into that furnace,
so that alight to your possibilities
we may pass the flame to others,
in our meeting, learning and sharing,
and together declare your unconfined presence.

Both babe and sibling

Charismatic Christ,
help us to recognise you in ourselves.
May you be both babe and sibling to us
as we explore our own growth and development.
May the face that shines from the manger
be the face we recognise each morning
whether we are down and out or on the up.

My body

This is my body,
the only one I have.
It is not invulnerable,
rather a bag for jumbled feelings:
anger, hurt, fear, loneliness.
Tears are sometimes near the surface,
sometimes trapped way down deep.
This is my body,
sometimes brave and excited,
bursting with energy,
lively and bubbling with enthusiasm.
I am full of life when
I can rock between all of these emotions,
visiting each one at the right time and place.
This is my body,
shared with others,
balanced on the edge,
seeking full and fruitful life.
This is my body,
made by the Creator,
shared by Christ,
refreshed by the Spirit.

Balance

Companion Christ,
present in dark and light,
there when the doubts come,
when the silences cannot easily be broken,
in your company I balance on the edge.
As we continue this way,
a route you know well
and one you have called me to,
still I hesitate to name death and face it.
You, who have been beyond the edge

so many times and in such diverse circumstances,
help me to hold my fears and name them,
to know that balance is not everything,
and to feel the way forward
to find a place where life returns.

Turning the tanker round

Almighty God,
in the channels of change,
as we struggle to turn the tanker round,
we need your strength with us
when our own efforts seem so puny
and the swell so deep.
Challenge us again,
in that small voice,
so easily swamped by the gale,
that we may realise and rejoice
that each healthy gust
is your Spirit tugging at us,
as we bob up again in the surf,
directing us towards your horizon.

The escalator of change

Companion Christ,
as I travel the escalator of change
keep in step with me.
It helps little to see you coming back the other way,
passing on the outside,
goading from behind
or heckling from in front.
It is only in the certainty
that you share this stairway
that I can cope with the ups and downs
that emerge from joining your journey.

Losing it

Don't give up on me, God!
I know I don't pray much, if at all really.
I admit I've drifted away, lost touch, lost interest.
But the chips are constantly down,
the deadlines notoriously short,
the pressure predictably high
and it's only the knowledge
that the shared cup and the late night call
are signs you are still hanging in there
that means I have not lost it either.

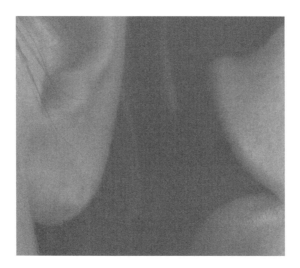

ALL CHANGE

Confession

If only it would, God.
If only it could, God.
If only change would and could be
the life-giving transition we all seek
in one easy-to-open package.
Forgive us when, with what we imagine
may be our last gasp,
we are unable to grasp
the spine-tingling, cell-dividing,
galaxy-whirring, asteroid-colliding,
enormity of what
'all change' really means to your body.

Assurance of pardon

Listen to this, people of God!
Jesus came to change things:
    to heal the sick;
    to teach the unlearned;
    to challenge the powerful;
    to live with those on the edge.
He says to us, as to others who responded to him:
'Go in peace. Faith changes life.'

CYCLE OF LIFE 2

Void

All-Knowing Nothing, All-Being No One,
how can you really be there;
hold the universe in your embrace?
I can't even shout or rage in this vacuum,
such is my emptiness.
Take it: it's all I have.
Then everything will have been given over.
I don't know any more if I even remain.

Worn down

Look at these elbows: scuffed.
Look at these cuffs: frayed.
Look at these hands: empty.
Look at this life: powerless.
I am worn down and worn out,
unable to believe that you might have been there too.
Show me the elbows, the cuffs, the hands, the life.

Exclusion

Left out again.
Still on the edge.
Ignored, excluded, abandoned
as if naked and totally vulnerable.
I fling my arms out in despair, *(do this now)*
my chest heaving.
As I do, maybe I'll catch a glimpse
of your mirror image.

Resistance

At least I can be angry:
keep me company, furious Creator.
At least I can dissent:
keep me company, protesting Christ.
At least I can rebel:
keep me company, revolutionary Spirit.
Holy Three, in your outrageous company,
may my resistance be tempered like steel.

Crucible

Persistent God, thankfully
the signs of life are all around me,
contributing to my growth and well-being.
Now I am being lifted up.
Whatever the wasteland, there's always something growing.
Like a scrawny shrub I cling to God, the Rock,
and will not be shaken.

Regenerate

Beyond the scratched surface we seek restoration.
In the wasteland we hope for the rebuilding of community.
Healing Spirit, we recognise that we do not require the quick fix,
but the sustaining flow of vision and energy
that comes from the Holy One and makes for wholeness.

Abundance

Now the river flows and the reservoir brims over.
Now the order book is full and the company thrives.
Now confidence grows and personality flourishes.
Now, Creator, we experience your energy at full strength
and we play happily as it showers on us.

Self-satisfaction

Another yawn stifled:
Great God, are you bored too?
Another day over:
Timeless One, do you not count them?
I seem to think I've made it;
fulfilled all my potential,
with no more challenges to meet
this side of whenever.
If you are today, yesterday and forever
help me to see there's more
to life before death
than that with which I'm satisfied.

Decline

Going down, down, down:
whether sliding off or bottoming out,
it seems to be all downhill from here.
You, who also went down beyond life and back again,
be present in the absence,
be attentive in the apathy,
be watchful in the indifference,
keep the death vigil with me
until we rise again.

NOTES

1   The opening lines of a hymn by John L. Bell and Graham Maule in *Enemy of Apathy* (Wild Goose Publications 1988).
2   The prayers in 'Cycle of Life' were first published in *Shining Faces*, the Prayer Handbook for 2000–2001, United Reformed Church, used by permission.

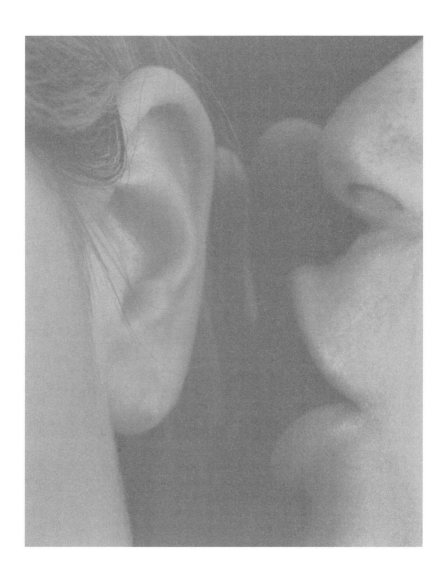

Chapter seven

Travelling on

Donkey day

Cross-marked beast you travel on your way.
Hear the people as they shout 'Hooray!'
Slowly, humbly, gentle too;
special, chosen for this job today.

Chorus
We will make the journey in your company,
bearing Jesus Christ for all to see.

Cross-marked church you wonder where to go,
to be faithful and just what to do.
Slowly dying, getting scared
wounds for faithfulness, all you can show.

Cross-marked beast you show us how to live,
we who feel we've nothing left to give,
travel on the palm-strewn way;
welcome one who fullest life will give.

Cross-marked church this road will never end.
Cross-marked hill is just around the bend.
Now the road is steeper still:
carry faithfully your loving friend.

Tune: Southcote (9979:119)

Each step, each hill, each street

As the world turns,
Creator keep you each day,
each step,
each hill,
each street.

As the people meet,
Christ keep you each day,

each step,
each hill,
each street.

As the energy flows,
Spirit keep you each day,
each step,
each hill,
each street.

May the Holy Three
watch and keep you each day,
each step,
each hill,
each street,
as you go on. [1]

Making peace

Peacemaker Christ
come and live with us.
Walk in our streets,
live in our homes,
so that each face we see
is recognised as your face
and each life we touch
recognised as your body.
By your look and your touch
may we know your peace.

Prayer on the doorstep[2]

They're 'changing rooms' on the telly,
and 'in my Father's house there are many',
but when the door is closed
to the only home I want,
wait on the new threshold with me.
[John 14:2]

The blue lagoon[3]

The blue lagoon
is not really blue:
more blueish green
or greenish blue.
In the same way,
silence is not golden
but rather a riot of colours,
as an artist's palette,
depending on whether,
for you it is

a prison
or an oasis,
a garden
or a jungle
or a deep,
    deep,
      deep
    deep
           well.

Sister Sophie [4]

Sister Sophie's sewing shirts for policemen;
    bobbin's bobbing,
    spool's spooling,
    wheel's whirring round.
So Sister Sophie's sewing shirts for policemen;
such soft striped shirts for policemen
Sister Sophie sews.
Now when you see a policeman
in one of Sister Sophie's shirts,
remember Sophie and her sisters
sitting sewing there;
    bobbin's bobbing,
    spool's spooling,
    wheel's whirring round.

The Church is a station [5]

The church is a station where trains just don't stop now:
wild flowers took over, there're leaves on the line.
They're still selling tickets and some tired old bread-cakes,
a bit of nostalgia, you can step back in time.

You can sit on the platform and dream of the good days,
when steam and then diesel all came this way.
It's hard to explain why it went out of fashion:
it's still good to visit for a quaint holiday.

Don't think you might just give your station a clean-up,
to try to keep up with a new modern trend
for chrome or for plastic or 'Thomas the Tank Engine'
or trendy cheap sarnies in buffets each end.

You'll meet lots of people who like to watch trains pass
who think that a station is fine for the view.
They never would use one for the purpose of travelling:
you must sit next to people, and of course you must queue!

There's a train that's still travelling, and still needs some stations
that are not just nostalgic or all gone to seed:
a station that's ready for all sorts of travellers,
despite their direction or what books they read.

God make us a station that's warm and inviting,
where trains run on time and there're places to go:
a station that's ready to respond to the moment,
when the signal goes up and whistle does blow.

Tune: Bard of Armagh (12.10.12.11)

Into silence

Take us into silence, God of all.
Embrace us with the silence
out of which the universe was made.
Challenge us with the silence
that greeted the prophets.
Caress us with the silence
that warmed Mary's womb.
Confront us with the silence
of the hostile crowds.
Energise us with the silence
of the Easter vigil.
Heal us with the silence
that vibrates through grief.
Confirm us with the silence
of the whispered name.
Forge us in the silence
of the Spirit's fire.

Still there

Even though the mist falls
I know the mountain is there.

Even though the wood is dense,
I know the cuckoo is there.

Even though the road is long,
I know the bothy [6] is there.

If I know these three;
    mountain,
    cuckoo,
    bothy,
how much more do I know you, God,
    creator of mountains,
    companionable cuckoo,
    and sheltering bothy.

'Space, place and grace – believing in the future' [7]

I believe in a god of space:
    one who created
    vastness from vastness
    and who calls each creature
    to find a space,
    both inside and out,
    to be at home.

I believe in a god of place:
    one who occupied
    a specific location,
    who accompanies each creature
    to find a place,
    in community,
    wholly themselves.

I believe in a god of grace:
    one who goes on giving,
    timeless source of energy,
    that renews each creature
    according to the basic
        rhythms of life.

I believe in continuing to believe.
I am committed to being a person of living faith
    in this space,
    in this place,
    by this grace.

Glory to god.

Travelling on

I travel on the open sea.
The waves mount;
I am carried upwards.
The gale roars;
I am tossed about.

I travel on the open sea,
where the albatross glides,
where the blue whale dives,
where the mackerel are schooling.

NOTES

1   For Bob's 'End to End', March–June 2003.

2   Written for Alma Brown, who spent the last 6 months of her life in hospital, three months of those waiting to 'go home' with appropriate home care help. She died two weeks after this prayer was written in June 2001.

3   The Blue Lagoon is east of Port Antonio on the north coast of Jamaica. This was written on a visit to Jamaica with members of St James and Shiregreen, Easter 2002.

4   'Sophie' and her sisters work at the garment factory run by the Mel Nathan Institute in Kingston, Jamaica.

5   First appeared in *Reform*, the magazine of the United Reformed Church, February 2005, page 29.

6   A small rural dwelling, like the one we stayed in on the Isle of Eigg where this was written in June 2005.

7   A. Davey, *Urban Christianity and Global Order*. London: SPCK (2001), page 124.

References/Bibliography

These are some of the publications that have influenced the writing of this book ...

J. Alison, *Faith Beyond Resentment: Fragments catholic and gay*. London: Darton Longman Todd (2001).

K. Baker-Fletcher, *Sisters of Dust, Sisters of Spirit: Womanist wordings on God and creation*. Minneapolis: Fortress Press (1998).

T. Beattie, *The Last Supper According to Martha and Mary*. London: Burns and Oates/Continuum (2001).

M.A. Beavis (ed), *The Lost Coin: Parables of women, work and wisdom*. London: Sheffield Academic Press (2002).

L. Byrne, *The Journey is My Home*. London: Hodder and Stoughton (2000).

K. Coffey, *Dancing in the Margins: Meditations for people who struggle with their churches*. New York: Crossroad Publishing (1999).

A. Davey, *Urban Christianity and Global Order.* London: SPCK (2001).

V.J. Donovan, *Christianity Rediscovered: An epistle from the Masai*. London: SCM Press Ltd (1982).

P. Freire, *Pedagogy of the Oppressed* (Revised edition). New York: Continuum (1993).

R. Harvey (ed), *Wrestling and Resting*. London: CCBI (2000).

W.R. Herzog, *Parables as Subversive Speech: Jesus as pedagogue of the oppressed*. Louiseville, Kentucky: Westminster/JohnKnox Press (1994).

D.R. Kendall, *Allegories of Heaven: an artist explores the 'Greatest Story Ever Told'*. Carlisle: Piquant (2002).

M. Kennedy (ed), *The Courage to Tell*. London: CCBI (1999).

A. Kramer-Dahl, 'Reconsidering the notions of voice and experience in critical pedagogy', in *Feminisms and Pedagogies of Everyday Life*, edited by Carmen Luke. New York: State University Press, pp 242-262 (1995).

M. Ledwith, 'Community work as critical pedagogy: re-envisioning Freire and Gramsci': *Community Development Journal*, 36: 171-182 (2001).

L.O. Macdonald (ed), *In Good Company*. Glasgow: Wild Goose Publications (1999).

C.C. Neuger, *Counselling Women: A narrative pastoral approach*. Minneapolis: Fortress Press (2001).

G. Philpott, *Jesus is Tricky and God is Undemocratic: The kindom of God in Amaoti*. Pietermaritzburg: Cluster Publications (1993).

D. Soelle, *Against the Wind: Memoir of a radical Christian*. Minneapolis: Fortress Press (1995).

M. Taylor, *Poverty and Christianity*. London: SCM Press Ltd (2000).

P.V. Taylor, *The Texts of Paulo Freire*. Open University Press: Buckingham (1993).

G. Thornburgh (ed), *That All May Worship*. An interfaith welcome to people with disabilities. Washington: National Organisation on Disability (1996).

J. Vincent and C. Rowlands (eds), *Bible and Practice*. British Liberation Theology, volume 4. Sheffield: Urban Theology Unit (2001).

H-R. Weber, *The Book that Reads Me: A handbook for Bible study enablers*. Geneva: World Council of Churches (1995).

G.O. West, 'Reading the Bible Differently: Giving shape to the discourses of the dominated'. *Semeia*, 73, 21–41 (1996).

G.O. West, *The Academy of the Poor: Towards a Dialogical Reading of the Bible*. Sheffield: Sheffield Academic Press (1999).

E. Wolde, *Ruth and Naomi*. London: SCM Press Ltd (1997).

About the author:

Janet Lees is a speech therapist and minister of the United Reformed Church. Her current research listening to the views of parents from marginalised groups concerning children learning to talk is based at the University of Sheffield, where she is an honorary lecturer. An honorary research fellow at the Institute of Child Health, University College, London, and a former writer and editor of the United Reformed Church Prayer Handbook, she has spoken and written extensively about contextual Bible study, disability, the history of the ordination of women in the United Reformed Church and children learning to talk, amongst other things. She lives in Sheffield with her husband and daughter.

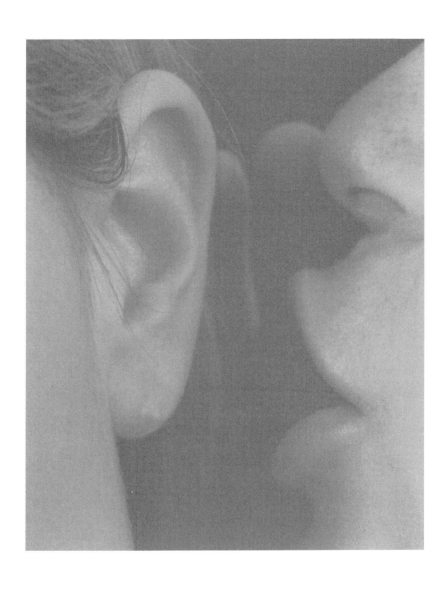

The Iona Community is:

- An ecumenical movement of men and women from different walks of life and different traditions in the Christian church
- Committed to the gospel of Jesus Christ, and to following where that leads, even into the unknown
- Engaged together, and with people of goodwill across the world, in acting, reflecting and praying for justice, peace and the integrity of creation
- Convinced that the inclusive community we seek must be embodied in the community we practise

Together with our staff, we are responsible for:

- Our islands residential centres of Iona Abbey, the MacLeod Centre on Iona, and Camas Adventure Centre on the Ross of Mull

and in Glasgow:

- The administration of the Community
- Our work with young people
- Our publishing house, Wild Goose Publications
- Our association in the revitalising of worship with the Wild Goose Resource Group

The Iona Community was founded in Glasgow in 1938 by George MacLeod, minister, visionary and prophetic witness for peace, in the context of the poverty and despair of the Depression. Its original task of rebuilding the monastic ruins of Iona Abbey became a sign of hopeful rebuilding of community in Scotland and beyond. Today, we are about 250 Members, mostly in Britain, and 1500 Associate Members, with 1400 Friends worldwide. Together and apart, 'we follow the light we have, and pray for more light'.

For information on the Iona Community contact: The Iona Community, Fourth Floor, Savoy House, 140 Sauchiehall Street, Glasgow G2 3DH, UK. Phone: 0141 332 6343 e-mail: ionacomm@gla.iona.org.uk; web: www.iona.org.uk

For enquiries about visiting Iona, please contact: Iona Abbey, Isle of Iona, Argyll PA76 6SN, UK. Phone: 01681 700404 e-mail: ionacomm@iona.org.uk

Wild Goose Publications, the publishing house of the Iona Community established in the Celtic Christian tradition of Saint Columba, produces books, tapes and CDs on:

- holistic spirituality
- social justice
- political and peace issues
- healing
- innovative approaches to worship
- song in worship, including the work of the Wild Goose Resource Group
- material for meditation and reflection

If you would like to find out more about our books, tapes and CDs, please contact us at:

Wild Goose Publications
Fourth Floor, Savoy House
140 Sauchiehall Street,
Glasgow G2 3DH, UK

Tel. +44 (0)141 332 6292
Fax +44 (0)141 332 1090
e-mail: admin@ionabooks.com

or visit our website at
www.ionabooks.com
for details of all our products and online sales